Ring Around the Moon

A celebration of life's simple pleasures

Lois Erisey Poole

To Linda
Life is magical!
Enjoy it!
Love
Lois Erisey Poole

PINCUSHION PRESS
CALIFORNIA

FIRST EDITION

Publisher's Cataloging in Publication
(Prepared by Quality Books, Inc.)

Poole, Lois Erisey.
   Ring Around the Moon : a celebration of life's simple pleasures / Lois Erisey Poole.
   p. cm.
   Preassigned LCCN: 96-70132
   ISBN 0-9653507-0-3

   1. Essays.   I. Title.

PS3566.O6654R56 1996   814'.54
                                  QBI96-40366

Printed in the United States of America

to
Mom and Dad
Their lessons are on every page.

Table of Contents

Foreword vii

Winter

January, Full Ice Moon 1

February, Full Wishing Moon 15

March, Full Narcissus Moon 25

Spring

April, Silver Cloud Moon.................... 37

May, Cabbage Rose Moon 49

June, Singing Cricket Moon 59

Summer

July, Full Thunder Moon 71

August, Full Peach Moon 83

September, Gray Owl Moon 95

Autumn

October, Full Pumpkin Moon 109

November, Red Leaf Moon................. 121

December, Full Snow Moon 127

Preface

*M*y father taught me that a ring around the moon was a sign of change. And I've learned that life, too, is circled with rings of change.

The joys of childhood roll into the fears and temptations of youth.

The pleasures of relationships flow into the weight of responsibilities.

The worry over careers revolves into pride as we progress along the pathway to our goals.

The dread of aging drifts to apathy of acceptance then glides into enchantment.

The grief at losing a dear one cycles into pleasure for having known them.

And finally the wisdom of age when we realize that time was a gift, life was priceless, and humor was the glue that melded these rings of change into appreciation.

So it is that each lifetime is woven into an intricate web of successes and failures that is shaped by changes as predictable as the changes foretold by a ring around the moon.

Lois Erisey Poole

Acknowledgements

I want to thank Jane Pikal who got me started; Linda Jackson Scott who believed in me; Ann Leddy Harris for pushing, prodding, and publishing; and my husband for giving me the space to complete this project.

But most of all, I want to thank my parents who instilled in me the desire to pursue a dream until it became reality.

Lois Erisey Poole

Winter

"I am grateful for what I am and have. My thanksgiving is perpetual. It is surprising how contented one can be with nothing definite—only a sense of existence."

Henry David Thoreau

January

Full Ice Moon

I've always thought it was a grand scheme to begin the new year with the month of January, the most difficult month of the year. January is a time that tests our stamina, sense of humor, and self-worth. It's a month of ice storms, white days, flu, frozen water lines and isolation. It prepares us for all the problems we will face in the coming year.

January - Northern Ohio - 1938
We buckled our boots, donned our woolen mackinaws, pulled on our stocking gloves, wrapped our knitted mufflers around our necks and shoveled a path through the great pyramids of snow to the chicken house. Surrounded by a still and silent world, the only sounds came from overburdened branches shrugging off their heavy white capes that fell to earth with a plunk and a flurry, startling the cottontails seeking ref-

uge below.

When we returned to the house, we removed our sodden clothes and draped them on chairs placed in front of the wall registers. Then we huddled by the fireplace, sipped tea, and reread *Little Women* or *Hans Brinker.*

After our bodies were restored, we dug through the shelves in the basement for the last jar of black-berry jam and heaved great chunks of coal into the overfed furnace which belched black smoke from its chimney.

The evening wind swirled the hard, white snow and swept it smooth. When we plodded to school in the morning, we searched for tracks of night visitors; rabbits and birds, or paw prints from a foraging 'coon. The frigid air made it difficult to breathe and our nostrils froze shut.

On the cold, dark January evenings we entertained ourselves by writing on the frosted windows while we watched the geese skate across the frozen pond. We worked jigsaw puzzles on the dining room table or played solitaire on the floor in front of the fireplace while we listened to Lux Radio Theater on the Philco.

We ate the last tangerines while Dad scanned the seed catalogs and dreamed.

Mom kept a pot of soup simmering on the back of the stove and yeasty breads baking in the oven.

We dug up cabbages, carrots, and turnips that had been buried in a pile of sand in the root cellar and snacked on snappy dill pickles from the crock that sat on the dirt floor beneath the Mason jars filled with fruit.

Dad carried in the first rings of browned sausage and slabs of pink bacon from the smokehouse.

We ate coffee soup, thick with cream and sugar, and chunks of buttered toast or we'd have crispy fried corn meal mush smothered in black apple butter while the cardinal, scarlet against winter's background, called its mate and dined with the chickens, and the nervous, iridescent pheasants searched the garden for forgotten ears of corn. Mice kept busy in the attic renovating their homes with the insulation they tore from the walls.

The snow shovel stood sentinel by the back door, not a flimsy aluminum thing but a heavy steel coal shovel that could lift great piles of snow from the walk with one scoop.

It was time for families to cluster together around the piano and sing of old Kentucky homes and long trails a-winding or the last rose of summer.

A time to pop corn and make fudge (which occasionally turned out).

A time to sit on the floor and try to crack enough black walnuts for a cake.

A time to huddle contentedly between soft blankets.

A time to watch and listen to the Northern Lights crackle and shimmer in a cold night sky, or count the falling stars.

A time of introspection and hibernation and security.

It was a time to be grateful for what we had because we had it all: shelter, food, a warm bed, and the comforting sounds of family small-talk lulling us to sleep.

§§§

*W*ithout a doubt, colds are a misery visited upon us by demon viruses! January seems to be the time of year when most of us go around speaking with a cork-stuffed-up-our-nose twang. And even though we have been told over and over by great minds that there are no dumb questions, I disagree. When I spend all day with a tissue under my nose, speaking in a hoarse whisper, my eyes tearing from an attack of painful coughing, it is *dumb* to ask, "Oh my! Do you have a cold?"

My chest has been trampled by overweight soldiers wearing army boots and my nose has been peppered with buck shot. My eyes have been sanded, and my lips feel and look as though they have been shingled with shake tiles.

The doctor assures me that these symptoms are not fatal.

I chill and turn up the heat to the screams of other family members who pointedly peel off their sweaters and wrinkle their noses at the aroma of menthol that permeates the house.

I'm not interested in life, but my common sense tells me this too will pass. But when? I don't believe that I won't die! I refuse to accept the fact that in a week or so my red nose will begin to peel, my cough will dissipate, and life will return to normal.

Fantasizing about my body invaders seems to help. I track billions of little viruses playing war games in my throat, chest and nose. I can sense when my immune system says "enough" and sends in an army of foot soldiers, camouflaged as white cells. The viruses fall in the trenches, their bodies piling up, and I am left to deal with their disposal.

I cough! I blow! My ears hurt! Food tastes like stale, moldy straw. A cup of hot tea brings on a flood from my sinuses and as I sip, I mop.

All wars are alike, aren't they? Some factions choose to be offenders. Some factions choose to be defenders. But it's always the innocent bystander who is left to clean up their mess.

❧❧❧❧

Several years ago I suddenly became very homesick for a garden, a plot of earth set aside for quiet meditation. We had a half acre area of unfenced, fallow land on the other side of the west lawn. So I began raking and clearing the land and burning piles of tumbleweeds and other debris that had accumulated over the years. Next I pruned all the trees that framed the area.

Then I planted flowering trees and shrubs, not in any grand pattern but here and there the way nature

5

plants her gardens. I slowly added bulbs, seeds, and vines. I scavenged the desert for discarded pieces of concrete left there by uncaring people who had eliminated patios to build pools, or driveways to add additions to their homes. Those smooth chunks of concrete were perfect to build paths throughout my haven. Then I dragged in huge fallen logs sculpted by time to add spots of interest. I placed benches here and there that I found at garage sales.

My husband built a trellis from old lumber and erected it at the end of one pathway; hung a swing in the old elm tree; put up a flag pole, and added a small concrete pool for all the wild things that pass through. I filled the trees with chimes and bird feeders and carefully placed bird baths and sun dials in the middle of the various small garden plots.

Everyone was skeptical except me.

"There's no way those plants will grow on the desert!"

"Your water bill will be horrendous."

"Too much work!"

But now, ten years later, my Open Garden is the conversation spot of the neighborhood.

It's a refuge of pleasure for all visitors and a safe harbor for the native wildlife and traveling dogs and cats who stop by for a drink and a short rest on a hot summer day.

In the spring my Open Garden rewards me with hundreds of daffodils and tulips, irises, hyacinths, and purple and white lilacs. Colorful anemones, ranunculus, freesias, columbine, and narcissus greet the day. The fragrance of the golden Spanish Broom undulates throughout the area like heat waves on an August road-way.

Later the garden glows with clumps of Shasta daisies, red and blue flax, and black-eyed Susans. The incandescent coreopsis casts its seeds flagrantly while the sophisticated red, orange, and peach day lilies nod sedately on June afternoons. All the roses and torch lilies thrive in the summer heat; and when the cool evenings of October arrive, the mums begin to burst forth with their rusts and whites and purples.

Finally, the last to bloom are the prolific, old-fashioned asters. Their blue-lavender daisy shaped flowers bend from the weight of the honeybees and butterflies drinking their fill before the cold of winter settles over the valley.

And then the trees change color and the leaves fall, carpeting plants with a warm winter coat, and suddenly one day the daffodils begin to peek through the earth and the cycle begins again.

And now my Open Garden is home to a family of kestrels who return each spring to build their nest and raise their noisy children. A red-tailed hawk bathes in the water dishes every morning at 10, and I wonder if she has a clock on the wall of her aerie. Edgy coyotes suspiciously watch over their shoulders as they lope down the paths and stop for a hurried drink while homeless cats, unaware of the predator, nap in furry balls on the benches, warm from the sun.

Mockingbirds eat the pyracantha berries and reward me with their night song. I sit on the old bench beneath the mimosa tree whose pink, feathery blooms wrap me in their perfume like a cape while the feisty hummingbirds dining from their sweet nectar dive-bomb my head with a squeaky warning that they will not share their feast with me.

On cold, January days I pause for a moment and drink in the fragrance of damp earth and decaying leaves and even though I'm swaddled in heavy clothes, I can sense the ghostly, gossamer days of spring lurking by the wall, those days when the pale blossoms of the fruit trees will be buzzing with honey bee activity.

My Open Garden is my private place, my quiet sanctuary of peace—my spiritual refuge where I feel nearer to God than any other place on earth.

❧❧❧

*W*inter is a strange time of year, isn't it? We get up in the dark and come home from our offices in the dark.

Our gardens become alien. We only see them on weekends when all the plants are brown and laced with frost.

I notice a few determined bulbs spiking leaves through the frozen earth. My hands itch to begin digging and planting. I pray that all my work from last summer will not be lost by the freezing mornings and cold, black nights.

Is there life there beneath that cold, hard earth? Will the oleanders shed those brown, dead leaves, and send forth new green ones? Will my hybrid irises survive and offer huge, pink, ruffled blossoms? Will my Open Garden glow with yellow daffodils again this spring? And the lilacs! How is it possible that those barren branches will become spears of fragrant purple stars begging to be smelled then picked?

Seed catalogs arrive daily. What promises they offer when I leaf through their colorful pages. I want to order everything! Try everything!

Faith! Faith not only moves mountains, faith creates wonderfully fragrant gardens, for gardens are nature's true promise for an abundant future.

꙰꙰꙰

I'm sitting in front of the fireplace listening to the logs crackle and the wind scuffling with the chimes strung along the eaves.

Tish, one of the terriers, is asleep by my side, and Sherwood, my cat friend, is curled on my lap interfering with my reading the pile of seed catalogs strewn across the coffee table in front of me.

These catalogs bring promises of vast platters of brilliant red tomatoes, crisp sticks of fried zucchini, and white, meaty baked potatoes.

It would be wonderful at this very moment if I could stroll to the garden and pick a purple globed eggplant, or pull a handful of long white radishes.

Such expectations and hopes are spread across the pages of these colorful brochures. But without hope and plans for the future, there would be no joy in life, would there?

I'm making out my order and putting out of my mind the future water bills, the tilling of the soil, the weeds, the necessity for fertilizers and compost, and the stiff, aching back. I'm trying to forget that just as the plants are ready to produce, the grasshoppers will invade searching for their midsummer feast. Perhaps though, this year, there will be a few summer showers, and just maybe the grasshoppers will find their summer staples elsewhere. For now, I'm planning!

Zucchini! Such a versatile vegetable. The small oval seed is planted in a hill, kept damp, and suddenly a small sprout appears. Gradually the sprout extends upward, developing dark, green leaves. These leaves, not unlike an umbrella, shade the fruit the plant will bear.

Zucchini bread! Spicy and fragrant from the oven. Moist and heavy when sliced and delicious when spread thickly with cream cheese.

If the fruit grows too large it can be halved, hollowed, stuffed and baked.

My favorite method for cooking zucchini is to pick small, green, tender ovals, slice them unpeeled, and place them in a casserole with a small, sliced onion, chopped fresh tomatoes, salt, pepper, butter, then sprinkle the top with Parmesan cheese, cover and bake in the oven until tender. With warm, crisp rolls this dish becomes a meal for the gods (or at the very least, gardeners).

Best of all, unlike chopping wood which warms me twice, my garden warms me three times: when I sit before the fire dreaming of what will be, when I till the soil and plant the seeds, and when I savor the harvest of my dreams.

❧❧❧

Sometimes I think too many of us look at the overall picture of our lives and ignore the candid shots of our lifetime. We must learn to love ourselves, especially as we age, and not look back with regret or forward with fear. We should cherish those moments that make up our lives, moments that have left indelible impressions.

That day we watched the sun slide below
 the horizon.
The first time our grandchild hugged us.
When we received that loving letter from
 home.
The gift of a perfect day.
Hummingbirds hovering at the feeders.
Sitting in front of a warm hearth on a blus-
 tery night.
A walk in the woods.
The rainbow's promise after yesterday's
 storm.
The luxury of a hot bath.

The smell of a basket filled with ripe apples.
The first glaze of purple on the lilac bush.
Opening a lacy valentine.
Playing cards with friends.
That day we stumbled upon a shimmering
    seashell.

Society measures success broadly, but success should be measured by those magical moments that sustain us as we wend our way through life. We must be cautious and never overlook momentary joys while we busily seek long-term pleasures. We need to reflect with passion upon those precious gifts of moments that can erase all regret for missed opportunities.

Everything ends. We retire from careers. Children grow up. Hobbies grow tiresome. Large homes become burdensome. But those treasured moments remain. They are the catalyst that makes our lives valuable.

❧❧❧❧

Winter has worn out her welcome at my home.
Her icy mornings have lulled me into submission. My body begs to stay under the warmth of the covers.

When I do bundle up and stagger to the kitchen, the terriers look up from their beds disgruntled, yawn, then go back to sleep.

Our cat Sherwood stands at the door, but when I

open it, shock filters across his face. He pivots and returns to his nest by the furnace.

Fickle winter spends her afternoons now teasing me with warm sunshine. She taunts me with a taste of what will be. And I foolishly accept her challenge just as she strikes with heartless force that sends me back to the blazing hearth and down comforters.

But today I noticed swollen buds on the mimosa tree. And the daffodils are sending up promises of gold. The pussy willow branches are filled with hope. The violets are opening their purple eyes and their fragrance dominates my Open Garden. A few narcissus have bloomed and the day lilies are awakening from their hibernation.

Winter is a time of rest. A time to restore energy to all living things. And soon the rest will be over. My Open Garden wants to grow—wants to bloom! And so do I.

꧁꧂

February

Full Wishing Moon

$\mathcal{T}$ onight, just after dark had settled over the valley, I walked outside and across the damp lawn. The terriers, Tish and Mac, bounded away barking at imaginary predators. They sniffed the grass as terriers will, accomplished their nightly toilette, then sipped water from the pond. While they were about their final business of the day, I glanced toward the sky. It was alight with stars. The Big Dipper shimmered and masses of twinkling lights adorned the black canopy.

Starlight!

We've read so much about starlight. Romantic songs spew forth its enchantment. The Three Kings followed it. Poets write esoteric words that proclaim its magic. But last night I saw the pine trees glow as the house cast a shadow from its incandescence. And I felt as though I were in a fantasy land of wonder.

Star light. Star bright.
First star I see tonight
I wish I may - I wish I might
Have the wish I wish tonight.

Splendor filled my heart at the end of this perfect day as I looked to God's heavens and saw the sky lit up like a giant landing field that no pilot could miss. And it was then, as the glow penetrated the darkness around me that I was filled with hope and knew that all my wishes for the future would be fulfilled.

❧❧❧❧

This month of February is proclaimed as the month of love. Bookstore shelves are laden with thin slick volumes devoted to the subject of love. How to love. When to love. Where to love. Who to love. The strains of certain songs evoke memories of impassioned longing so strong it is difficult to continue with the task at hand. We read philosophical essays about the strength of love and how this one emotion can over-come all adversity. But learning about the emotion of love is not the solution to life's problems, the solution to life's problems is recognizing the emotion of hate.

Hate is more powerful than love, more powerful than happiness. Hate is all consuming. To hate takes time and strength and saps us of all other feelings. When a heart is hardened with hate, that heart's entry is sealed against love, sealed against compassion and under-standing.

Hate produces offspring; envy, jealousy and greed. And when we permit hate to take up residency in our hearts we give our lives over to a tenacious beast who, like all parasites, will destroy its host.

But love—wonderful, symbiotic love will live with us and through us and for us. A heart filled with love will make our cheeks glow; our eyes gleam. Love brings a softness to the face, a kindness to the spirit, a pleasure to the soul.

We must work at leaving the entry to our hearts open so love can enter and we must sweep that entry clean every day so hate will never find room to survive and propagate. Through sharing, our love will grow and prosper. And only then will we find true happiness.

⋙⋘

As we grow older many of us become more flexible—more forgiving.

We are comfortable with God. We have reached the age of common sense about religion. We know now that everything is not black or white, cold or hot, because throughout our lifetime we discovered those many warm grays that instilled the calm in our lives.

Age erases embarrassment; dissolves shame. Suddenly what was traumatic becomes a good yarn to bequeath to our grandchildren. We have found peace with ourselves and with God. We have buried resentments, apologized for wrongdoings, and understand the errors of our past. Our days of repentance leave us with a pure mind and a clean conscience.

We feel secure in our knowledge that God has forgiven us all our youthful indiscretions and our middle-aged desires. Now, here we are, and we know that what is truly critical is to have learned throughout life to instill in the next generation the desire to be all that they can be and to promote the faith they will need to carry through their plans.

As we age, we slow down, not only physically but emotionally. We don't face as many crises in our lives because our priorities have changed. Stumbling blocks become small stones to be kicked gently from our path. Major issues dissolve into trivial pursuits. Worries fade. We succumb to an inner resolve of satisfaction—peace. We become one with nature.

We feel God's presence in the afterglow of a thunderstorm. We smell God in the fragrance of wet pine woods. We see Him in the light of a full harvest moon. We hear His voice in the rustle of the willow trees. We taste His sweetness in a sun-warmed peach plucked off a summer tree. And all the while we feel the pressure of His warm hand on our shoulder.

He is there—waiting. We are here—waiting. And one day the journey will be over. We will meet. And like good children, we must remember our manners. We must thank Him for this gift of life and for His book of instructions on how to assemble that life correctly.

ঌঌঌঌ

$\mathcal{T}$oday, even though the sun shines, the wind slashes rain against the south window.

The birds don't mind, though. They flock to the feeders and squabble and eat and dash to a tree and search the sky and drop to the ground and eat again. Birds are happy with the necessities of life; food, shelter, a branch to perch upon, a puddle of water for bathing.

Today they're splashing in the driveway. Splashing and shaking and washing away the winter dust.

A black-capped chickadee sat at the feeder outside the kitchen window and nervously ate while he guarded the food from his friends. Even birds can be greedy!

A storm is moving through from the north and when the cool air meets the warm air a great windstorm occurs. Tumbleweeds roll and the fragrance from the rain-soaked woodpile slides through the window and makes me pause for a moment.

I lift my head and sniff at the wonders of nature. I close my eyes and hear the mountain streams and smell the pine forests. Over there a deer stands looking for her mate. An otter quietly slips into the stream; a loon calls; a lone dove coos, her soft voice sensual in the morning air.

I rouse from my reverie and despite the intermittent rain I begin to prune the trees and plant some seeds. This immediately throws me into another dream sequence of a garden of plenty this summer.

Rows of purple cosmos and sweet pea vines thick with creamy flowers. My old cracked teapot sits on the kitchen table filled with fragrant white and pink roses.

The violets are blooming. "Shy violets" because they bloom within the foliage and are difficult to see. But their heavy perfume drifts across the garden and brings forth thoughts of romantic evenings glowing with candlelight and warmed by love.

But is love candlelight? A full moon? Romantic trysts?

I think love must be caring about others and things. Things like flowers and cacti and trees. Things like hummingbirds and Joshua trees and crickets.

Love is cooking a pot of chili on a cold winter's day.

Love is doing the laundry. Planting a flower. Scrubbing the floors.

Love is making a swing and hanging it from the tallest tree. And pruning the shrubs and picking a bouquet of wild flowers.

Love is sharing the last cup of coffee and fixing a flat tire.

Love is getting up early and turning up the heat so the house will be warm for the rest of the family.

Love is not complaining about an unmade bed, or a sink filled with dirty dishes, or a dusty house, or sandwiches again for dinner.

Love is evening's calm and the first blush of dawn.

Love is snowcapped houses and steaming, fragrant tea.

Love is a sleeping household, settled for the night.

Love is a smile and a hand on our shoulder.

Love is sharing all joys and sorrows with a friend.

Love is remembering and love is forgetting.

ë**ë**ë**ë**

Somehow the controlled perfection and delicate lines of the Bonsai tree disturb me. Every time I see a Bonsai that has been carefully tended, groomed, snipped, and shaped, I am reminded of absolute power over another living thing.

The Bonsai demurely sits in its flat dish where even its roots are trimmed beneath the soil —the better to maintain its tiny stature.

Man's objective is to stilt its growth, bind its roots, and imprison it in a small cell where it has no freedom to become what nature intended it to be.

Bonsai culture is an ancient art of the Orient, and perhaps one day this ancient art will become just another part of history. Until then I will not own a Bonsai nor will I shape my shrubs into grotesque caricatures of nature. Everything and everyone should be free to spread their branches and follow their own lifescript without interference.

But, happily, I notice that despite man's intervention he cannot control the inner spirit of the Bonsai. It keeps growing, attempting to reach its potential. And until man controls the heart of the Bonsai, man controls nothing at all.

⁂

*I*n this month that symbolizes love, I find that pressuring our children to have an idol is a dangerous activity. You know the sort of person I'm speaking of. The man who can do no wrong; the man who lives a pristine life; never swears; never commits a sin; a man who is kind to his parents, small children, and puppies?

We hear all the time how children must have a role model. But how difficult it is to be perfect all the time. No one is. Because all humans make mistakes.

Even Adam bit into the apple. Even Peter denied his Lord.

Preachers are an example of an idol so many of us put on a pedestal only to see the pedestal crumble and the man fall in a heap of human dust.

Politicians are another group we look up to. Many of us become such obsequious fools in their presence that we fail to see their obvious flaws.

Sports figures and entertainers have fans! And according to these overzealous fans their idols are flawless! Then suddenly when these fans discover their saint is just another human with human frailties, they are shattered. Some fans exhibit outrage while others foolishly overlook these foibles and continue their blind adulation.

And parents! Parents aren't perfect either. We parents can never hope to be a role model for our children. We make mistakes. We swear on occasion. We sneak the last piece of chocolate cake and hope no one sees. We fantasize about a beautiful neighbor. We pilfer a box of paper clips from the office. We stretch the truth on our tax forms. We overeat. We drink too much. We make fools of ourselves at the Little League field.

Maybe we should just teach our children to grow up under the philosophy of the Golden Rule and attempt to instill in them some common sense. Maybe then we would become a nation of relatively honest people, doing an honest day's work, for an honest day's pay. Everyone's idol should be a person they trust, a person filled with pride and a sense of self-worth. And that person should be themselves.

≈≈≈≈

March

Full Narcissus Moon

The wind is blowing!

Antagonists, cold air and warm air, have met and are fighting an angry battle for supremacy.

The persistent wind of the desert is battering the already-leaning trees and throwing dry twigs onto the lawn. The terriers' facial hair whips back, exposing eyes filled with black fright. They look at me, then frantically claw at the door, demanding entrance. The cypress tree, planted near the foundation of the house, hammers at the eaves, its trunk lacerated from the conflict.

Daffodils are tattered and limp from this unleashed wrath. Sand from our unpaved road picks up tumbleweeds, discarded plastic containers and roofing shingles as it runs a mad marathon to nowhere.

Television reception has been interrupted, cars sway, motor homes are blown off the road, allergies are the topic of conversations, and we rush outside to batten down or bring in anything moveable until peace returns to the valley.

Residents of this Mojave desert attempt to find one redeeming virtue about the winds. Maybe nature is warning us that the natural growth of this land is strong and capable of withstanding her frenzied tantrums and bad temper. The shallow-rooted Joshua tree has stood for thousands of years, a beacon of stability on this raw terrain. Those of us who have attempted to transplant our Midwestern or Eastern influences onto this strange but beautiful desert must learn that nature comes in many guises. Only the tenacious survive here.

And while the sky is cleansed of all impurities a feeling of security settles over me. I'm thankful for minimal assets; shelter, a pot of stew simmering on the stove, a scarf to tie around my head.

And after a moment of reflection I appreciate even more the most valuable asset given to me—myself.

꒰ꂧ꒱ꂧ꒱

I've never been certain about an afterlife. Does it truly exist ? Or is it a nice story concocted to make us less fearful about death? I still don't know—no one really does. Great religious minds tell us what they believe but they don't really know. Anyway, I'd like to tell you my story and then you can decide for yourself.

When I was 5 years old, my brother, Johnnie, was

nineteen. He had a job and a car and a girlfriend. He was interested in everything. He practiced with a bow and arrow until he became proficient. He took flying lessons and got his pilot's license. He was eager to learn something new every day. He had a collection of muzzle-loading shotguns, collected arrowheads, took a correspondence course to better himself, and played the banjo and piano without benefit of sheet music.

He bought me candy bars, plunked me on his lap and combed my long hair, told me stories, and took me with him whenever he went someplace exciting.

Eventually, he married and had three children, but the tie we had was never broken. I loved him with a passion that is impossible to describe.

One warm, sunny March day, shortly before his 38th birthday, he died after a sudden, debilitating illness.

I felt deserted, lost, alone. But most of all I worried about him. Was he happy? Was he well? Was he truly living in that afterlife I'd been taught to believe existed?

About one month after he died, I had a dream.

I dreamed I was in bed and the doorbell rang. I went downstairs to answer it; and when I opened the door and went out onto the porch, Johnnie was standing at the bottom of the porch steps. He looked so happy and so well. His brown suit no longer hung from his shoulders but fit him like it was tailor-made. Humor filled his blue eyes and his curly hair was neatly combed.

I was so happy to see him. I cried, "Johnnie!" and started toward him. I wanted to hug him. He looked so well.

He stepped back and said, "No. You can't touch me. I came to tell you that I'm all right. I'm happy. Don't worry about me anymore. Get on with your life." With that he turned and walked down the sidewalk.

"Johnnie!" I called. "Wait!"

I felt someone pull me back and I looked down to see skeleton hands on my shoulders. They didn't frighten me. I simply knew they were death separating us.

Johnnie turned, smiled and waved good-by.

That dream brought me contentment and peace of mind. This took place in 1954 and I have never dreamed of him again. I did as he told me, I got on with my life.

❧❧❧

*T*he primrose is greening up, the calendula are in bud, and the owl "whooo whooo's" for a mate.

The doves bobble along the driveway eating the grain I have spread about and the jays scold and want it all for themselves.

Wind tosses the chimes and the sound casts music throughout the house.

It's still fireplace weather and the redwood logs crackle and emit a furious heat that turns toasting legs fire red.

A cup-of-tea-and-Emerson-essays weather.

A talk-with-a-friend weather.

And the time grows nearer to longer days and the white hollyhock blooming by the fence.

Soon the tamarack tree will blossom into a pink cloud in my Open Garden, and the poinciana tree will bloom its fragrant yellow and red flowers. Another cycle will have come full circle.

Cycles of weather and people and wars continue.

We never seem to expect cycles in our lives. We always appear surprised at a sudden rainstorm or a morning after a snowfall.

We are alarmed when war is declared.

We're shocked when a friend dies.

But all of these happenings occur as a matter of course. They should be expected. They're a part of the cycle of life, of seasons, of people.

Instead, we should be surprised when the apple tree blooms in the fall; when a friend fails us; when a parent deserts us. These are not normal developments, not events we should expect.

Actions that oppose the norm should always bring surprise otherwise we become cynics—always expecting the worst. And cynical people are not messengers of joy.

❦❦❦

I'm homesick for the simplicity of life. The smell

of coffee boiling on the stove, a bowl of fresh picked peonies, new mown hay, milk —warm and foamy from the bucket, eggs from the nest, and the challenge of popping homegrown popcorn.

I miss evenings on the porch watching lightning bugs flicker in the hollow, and searching for the man in the moon while licking the paddles of the ice cream maker. I miss home-bottled root beer exploding in the basement, sauerkraut from the crock, wine siphoned from the barrel and catching frogs in the stream.

I miss Mom and Dad, voices low in the kitchen, making all the decisions and sharing the responsibilities while I play with my paper dolls on the living room floor.

I want to watch the Lionel train chugging along the tracks under the Christmas tree while the smell of gingerbread floats throughout the house.

I want to pick wild strawberries, gather violets, walk in the woods, wade in the stream and come home to lemonade and sugar cookies waiting on the kitchen table.

I'd like to shop again at the grocery store where Mr. Burns sliced cheese from a wheel, wrapped it, then ran a credit tab with the pencil stuck behind his ear. I'd like to smell homemade lye soap, blackberry jam simmering on the coal stove and bread baking in the oven.

I long for those snowbound days spent in drawing pictures with my fingers in the frost that gathered on the inside of the windows, eating apples sprinkled

with salt, crisp fat-rimmed pork chops, and corn slath-
ered with butter.

I want to hear coal sliding down the makeshift
chute and crashing onto the cellar floor. And choose
from the basement shelves a shining jar of peaches or
pears; meat or beets; jam or catsup.

I want to step up on the porch and pause for a
moment as I absorb the aroma of baking bread ac-
companied by the comforting sound of rattling pans
that floats through the screen door.

I am a product of two eras; a member of the lucky
generation. I have freedoms today brought about by
the discovery of complicated systems of electronics
and labor-saving devices unimagined by my parents,
and I also have memories of those technologically free
days of my childhood. But I get homesick.

Homesick for the uncomplicated joy that was
found in those carefree days spent eating windfall
apples.

Homesick for the rope swing that hung from the
maple tree.

Homesick for those snow-covered hills of home
where one day I stood and knew life would always be
that safe and that happy and that simple.

❧❧❧

I don't care what the experts say! I don't care
if my fireplace wastes heat! I don't care if it causes
cold drafts that spin across the floor and spiral up the

chimney! I don't care if it creates a mess of feathery gray ashes or occasionally discharges a puff of smoke that rises to the ceiling! I don't care if the logs house a spider, drop bark on the rug, or come filled with termites! A house is not a home if it doesn't have a fireplace! A fireplace is a home's core—its heart!

The comfort and security that come from a blazing hearth is a feeling as old as time. Perhaps it's the caveman instinct, but life is more fulfilling and cheery when one sits before a crackling fire sipping tea and discussing the joys of life with a dear friend.

At Christmas my mantel is glorious with our collection of antique Santas buried in fir boughs gathered from our yard. It's this moment that fills me with sadness for those unfortunate folks who don't have a mantel to decorate at Christmas and a roaring fire beneath to feed their souls.

I don't want a gas log in my fireplace. I don't want to burn those foolish little paper covered sawdust things available at the supermarket. I don't want to toss in a handful of kindling. I want big, flaming logs snapping and throwing their heat across the room; logs that burn for hours.

Seductively, the fire whispers, "Come. Stand by my side where I can hug you with my warmth."

And no one is capable of overcoming its allure; we all surrender to its enchantment. The first chair guests take is the one by the fire. Other folks stand before the hearth, legs growing red and itchy from the heat.

I remember an Ohio bedroom where ice formed on the inside of the windows. I remember the security of Dad telling me (ordering me), not to leave the warmth of my bed until the fire was stoked and heat had emanated throughout the rooms. I remember walking down the oak staircase and standing before the fireplace with its iron grate filled with hot-orange chunks of coal. I dressed there while the winter wind drifted the snow across the driveway, isolating us from the world. The comfort of knowing I was loved, and the wisdom to remember that warm, secure feeling has sustained me throughout my life.

Leave my fireplace alone!

❧❧❧

Today I walked through my Open Garden and paused for a few moments beneath the old locust tree. Its clusters of snowy flowers cascaded from the gnarled branches and their fragrance drifted across the garden.

I noticed, as I sat down on a bench, that the oldest trees in my garden are the most beautiful. Their twisted branches hug each other lovingly as the patina of age shimmers from their rugged trunks.

These trees have endured fierce wind storms, insect invasions, and lightning strikes. Some bear scars from children attempting to cut them down with toy saws. They have character burrowed into their ragged bark. And if they could speak, they could tell enchanting tales.

The Joshua tree, hundreds of years old, could surely tell us of the Indian family who spent the night beneath its ghostly branches planning their trip at dawn.

The fragrant mimosa could recount the hopes of the young couple who dug the hole for its virgin roots.

The elm, persisting through drought and wind, could relate the secret of the carved heart, long since healed into a silver scar.

Even the birds prefer the craggy old trees for nesting and scolding. A mockingbird, perched on one knobby branch, threatened me and ordered me to be gone.

My shaggy trees, sculpted by the wind and seared by the sun, have roots that are deep and solid, unlike the smooth saplings which have not yet seen enough of life to have the radiant beauty that the venerable trees impart. The old trees stand as an indisputable beacon toward the joys of aging.

It seems the older the tree, the more graceful, the more valuable it becomes. And I can't help but reflect that our society protects and reveres everything that is old except its people.

Perhaps if we altered our perceptions of beauty to include ourselves as we age and placed a higher value on our accomplishments, we would find greater contentment. And if we would instill anticipation for the progression of aging as a goal rather than a process to be feared, all people of all ages would benefit from our resolute and inspiring attitude.

Spring

"Heaven is under our feet as well as over our heads."

Henry David Thoreau

April

Silver Cloud Moon

*L*ately, I have been thinking about how difficult it is for some people to cry. Showing emotion, particularly when tears are involved, seems to be an embarrassment—something to choke back and hide.

And I have been pondering what makes me cry. Animal movies are one. It seems these movies always have as their theme a cruel owner, or a lost animal suffering horrendous abuse before the story ends happily. And during the traumatic climax I become a blubbering mass. I refuse to watch animal stories now because I'm upset for days. And I can't help but wonder what the poor star had to endure in order to present such a convincing performance.

Thoughts also bring tears to my eyes. Thoughts of my parents, gone now, and my family who live on the other side of the country; the times I became angry at my children when they were toddlers; words spo-

---

ken that can never be taken back; guilty feelings of past omissions and commissions. I find that my emotional stability is a good reason to never think of the past. The past is done with and nothing will ever change what happened yesterday.

I also feel tearful when I walk through second-hand shops and find lovely old dishes or handmade doilies sitting on tables waiting to be bought by a collector. And I wonder why children can't find one small spot in their grand homes to save these items to hand down to their children and their children's children. There is a lifescript written in each dish or piece of tattered lace, lifescripts that should never be destroyed, given away, or sold. I think of the tears that may have been shed over this bowl while a grandma was mixing a batch of cookies, or tears of happiness when a mother crocheted the edge on that baby dress. These things are too personal, too private to be placed in the home of a stranger.

And I cry when I lose a pet. This past weekend I lost my little Sophie. She was 17 years old and had been a faithful friend and companion. When her days were finally darkened and silenced with blindness and deafness, I knew it was time.

I buried her in my Open Garden and planted a yellow iris, my favorite flower, upon her little grave. And now when I go to the garden to sit awhile, she's by my side, snapping at the water, barking at intruders, and exuding love from her little terrier body.

Sophie deserves my tears, my sadness, my mourning at her passing. The unconditional love and joy she gave to me during those 17 years will remain in my heart forever.

❧❧❧

*M*y house has become a health hazard; a perilous, unsafe corner of the world. I never realized its potential for danger until my 4-year-old granddaughter arrived for a visit.

The first thing she picked up was the scissors and ran to show me her find. I retrieved the weapon and after my heartbeat returned to normal I scavenged the house for pills, needles, pins, matches, knives, and bug spray.

Suddenly I was forced to check the water temperature for repeated hand washings; turn the pot handles to the back of the stove; barricade the cupboard doors that contained the cleaning supplies, and remove the contents from all the candy dishes.

Glass drinking glasses had to be replaced with plastic.

Plastic bags were discarded, and cactus plants were relocated to unavailable corners of the house.

All my newly planted seeds were flushed into the neighbor's yard when demands to help water the garden were yielded to.

When I walked into the kitchen, I discovered six cookies lying about the countertops with one bite removed from each. A Popsicle stick had adhered to a kitchen chair, crayons rolled dangerously across the floor, and the cat refused to come out from beneath the bed.

Grandpa came up behind me and between sneezes, whispered through clenched teeth, "Hide that spray can of air freshener!"

I watched Cinderella so many times I wanted to pick up that glass slipper and knock some sense into that vacant cavity where her brain was supposed to be. Besides, where was my Fairy Godmother when I needed her most?

I read Bambi until I had it memorized, and I determined that Barney was purple because a grandma, someplace, had attempted to choke the life out of him!

I became a victim of tantrums.

The cat (who finally got hungry) and I mopped up the milk after she insisted that she didn't need help pouring it over her cereal.

I replaced the seedlings after she assured me she could handle a rake.

I picked up the alphabet cards after my threats were met with resistance.

I washed the walls after it was discovered they were more fun to paint than those silly paper pictures.

My back ached from running alongside a tiny bicycle as it wobbled its way up and down the driveway, and my knee was bruised where the swing banged into it.

I felt like a young mother again and quite frankly I didn't like the feeling. After all, I've been there— done that! But when I discovered the garish red spot from spilled, smuggled fruit drink permanently decorating my new white area rug I decided that God knew what he was doing when He equipped females with eggs that are programmed to destruct after the age of 45.

❧❧❧❧

*T*he fruit trees in my Open Garden are in bloom!

Last night, under a full moon, I walked to the garden where the blossoms reflected the moonlight, creating an ethereal moment. I was met with a mystical vision of white and pink balloons that had just landed. I watched to see if my unicorn would appear and crop the violets, or if a meadow faerie might fly past and wave her translucent wing in greeting.

The night air held just enough moisture for the blossoms to emit a delicate fragrance, a fragrance that reminded me of plump peaches, sweet plums, and crisp almonds.

The beauty of nature transcends all other beauty on earth. When we were given this wonderful gift of life it was a package deal. We were given clouds and rainbows, smells and colors and sounds, so we could enjoy the total art of being. For what else does one need? Where else is such beauty found? What else do we need to sustain us through this exciting journey we have embarked upon?

Last night I listened to the mockingbird sing his night song while Pan played his pipes and tranquillity settled over my world.

❧❧❧❧

&pitaphs tell a story; a history of what occurred yesterday. They tell how people felt about one another, and many times they tell the sort of life the deceased lived. Epitaph is a Roman word that means, "Stay, passer by." Epitaphs are more honest than eulogies. Eulogies are generally grandiose talks spoken to impress the audience rather than true facts compiled to outline the deceased's life. Overflowing with sentimental phrases, delivered in a melancholy voice, eulogies can be depressing and riddled with falsehoods, but epitaphs are from the heart. Their few lines speak volumes and make the reader think.

History tends to become distorted depending upon its author. We can read many books and derive opposite renditions on the same subject, but epitaphs never change. They can not be altered by man or time. They are carved in granite or stone. They're permanent lifescripts etched for eternity.

It seems that today epitaphs have become a thing of the past, and yet many were inscribed with such love and left such a potent legacy that they might be worthy of consideration in the present time.

"Here Lies Mary Dawson. She Died Before Her Time." And beneath, scratched into the marble, are the dates 10-3-1868 4-2-1889. Mary Dawson was obviously a young woman of 21 when she died. Why did she die? Was she married? Could she have died in childbirth? Or from an epidemic that assaulted the county?

"Our Little Jennie Brown. Now She Plays With The Angels." 3-8-1798 to 5-6-1798. Little Jennie was 2 months old. Her parents must have been heartbroken. Beside Jennie's grave is another marker: "Baby Boy Brown. Your Mother Loved You." 2-8-1796. Only one date. Did the baby die at birth? Was he Jennie's brother? How did those parents, losing two children in 2 years, cope with their loss? Did they have other children who reached adulthood?

"Here Lies Old Bill Jackson. Surely Burning In Hell." Well! That tells us all about the life of poor Old Bill! He must have been a rascal or worse.

Occasionally, people ask me what I would like my epitaph to say. And I respond that I want my epitaph to read, "Here Lies A Woman Who Finished What She'd Begun. Life Has Many Roads, She Traveled Every One."

<center>~~~~~</center>

Spring is the friendliest time of the year. I grow weary of cold weather; lighting the fires, adjusting the furnace, gathering up the heavy coats and gloves, and scraping ice off the car windows every morning. Even the terriers take to their beds and look at me with shock when I suggest they go outdoors for their morning or late evening hiatus.

But one day lovely Spring tiptoes down the road and quietly passes through our back gate and sprinkles the lawn with green "hello's."

The buds on the trees swell with welcome, and the wintered bulbs awaken and slowly push through the damp, cool earth.

There is warmth around the edges of the days. The sun is a little brighter. The birds begin to sing. The terriers grow alert and playful. I want to clean the house and take the blankets from the beds. The rooms are stuffy, the walls are yellowed with winter's grime, the curtains are limp, and everything needs to be renewed, freshened, and scrubbed clean.

The garage must be swept out, and the heavy coats and boots beg to be stored. I walk through the garden to see if everything survived its winter hibernation.

I tend to leave the doors open now when I pass through, if only for a few moments, capturing the aroma of the warming earth. I recall a line from Song of Solomon, "... *the flowers appear on the earth, the time of singing of the birds is come, and the voice of the turtle is heard in our land.*"

Winter often enters through the front door, slamming and ordering us about before we have readied the impedimenta for survival. Summer can descend as suddenly as a swooping eagle, holding us in his hot talons for months. Autumn, more like her sister, Spring, can be a welcome guest, too. Autumn comes to visit, cool, polite and satisfying. But it is Spring, lovely Spring, who enervates and revives us.

Spring is a backdoor guest. She brings gifts: bowls of golden daffodils, redheaded finches, fragrant star-flow-ered lilacs, gray-breasted doves. She also brings changes to our lives with her bright days and soft breath. And like any good guest—she never stays long enough to wear out her welcome.

❧❧❧❧

So many people respond to "And how was your day?" with, "Oh, same old thing," making it sound as though every day is the same, but I've noticed that every one of my days is different.

For example, last Monday the scarlet flax bloomed! Its red stars dominated the garden and hummingbirds found its nectar to be especially tasty as they darted from flower to flower and dive-bombed my head, warning me away from their gourmet dinner.

On Tuesday the bantam hen hatched all fourteen of her eggs. The bundles of black and yellow flitted in and out from under Mother, who was exceptionally agitated over tending such a large, unruly brood.

On Wednesday my friend called to say her test results were in and that she would be fine. This was wonderful news related to me by a kind, caring person who has known ill health for years, yet is always there for others.

On Thursday I was attacked by a particularly nasty bug which was intent upon destroying my inner being with vicious assaults. But true to form, I rose up and became the victor in this nasty little twenty-four-hour battle.

On Friday morning I walked to the kitchen and saw

a Western tanager at the bird feeder. Its bright red, yellow and black coloring was startling against the gray dawn. I was still feeling a little weak from Thursday's attack, but this gift given to brighten my day was accepted with grace. I immediately felt stronger.

On Saturday my sister called from Kansas just to say hello; my friend called to get a report on the outcome of Thursday's combat, and all the roses suddenly bloomed! The terriers discovered a mouse living under the woodpile and noisy excitement ran rampant for an hour or so. The hummingbirds renovated their nest on the front porch, and my husband and I painted the lawn furniture.

On Sunday my cousin phoned from Ohio. I hadn't heard from him for many years. Speaking to a long-ago friend and childhood ally awakened so many remembrances of times past and thoughts of growing-up pleasures.

So I can't help but wonder if the reason we respond to "how was your day?" with "same old thing" isn't because we just don't pay enough attention to the blessings that surround our everyday lives.

Is there more to life than watching the birds squabble at the feeders? Or sipping a cup of tea before the fire? Or smelling a fresh rose? Or finding a gnarled root carved by time? Or a touch on the shoulder as a loved one passes by our chair? All of these things *are* life.

Too many of us fret about the past, worry about the

future and miss the present—the now of life. How can every day be the same when each day is so filled with surprises and the simple pleasures that make living worthwhile?

🍂🍂🍂🍂

Spring on the Mojave desert is Joshua trees in bloom.

It's the returning hummingbirds, and a lost robin singing from the chinaberry tree.

It's thunderous black clouds in the west bidding hello to a rosy dawn.

It's tender nights, and fierce, afternoon winds.

Spring on the desert is fields of orange poppies and cackling ravens.

It's rattlesnakes moving out of hibernation to warm in the sun and cat fights under bedroom windows.

It's mud-between-the-toes evenings and weeds in my Open Garden.

It's mockingbirds singing all night from the sweet locust tree.

Spring on the desert is the fragrance of lilacs, and blooming orchards.

It's the joy of longer days ending with moonlight walks amid clumps of daffodils.

It's the comfort of a pleasant night's rest after a day in the garden.

It's the sound of tractors and lawn mowers and

chain saws.

Spring on the desert is a bid good-bye to the bleakness of winter.

It's new beginnings and future plans and dreams fulfilled.

It's painting time and cleaning time and weeding time and walking time.

It's life springing green on brown mesas and love returning to fallow hearts.

❧❧❧

May

Cabbage Rose Moon

All Right! I know!

I know my house needs a thorough cleaning.

I know all the walls need to be painted.

I know all the books on the shelves need to be dusted.

I know I have too much stuff around the house and that I need to get rid of some of it.

I know that doilies are old-fashioned.

I know, because my kids love to remind me at every visit how dated and dusty my house really is.

"Mom, you really need to paint this kitchen. It's getting so yellowed."

"Gosh, Mom, this place looks like a Hallmark store!"

"Mom! It's summer! Don't you think it's time to take the wreath off the front door?"

"Good heavens, Mom. Don't you ever close

---

those drapes?"

"Good grief, Mom! I hope you never move! I'd hate to have to help you pack up all this stuff!"

Then visitors arrive. Their eyes scan my house and I can see shock flitter across their faces. Occasionally a brave soul remarks, "You sure do have a lot of stuff, don't you!"

Now I want you to understand that my house is clean. I dust and polish and scrub just the same as everyone else. I even have a woman who comes in now and then to clean. However, I do have a lot of stuff.

But I've reached an age where if I want a wreath on my front door all year 'round it will be on my front door all year 'round.

I now become stiff after I've spent a day on a ladder so I plan to paint this summer when the weather is warm and the furnace is off.

As for the books? I'm just too busy watching the birds and talking to the daisies to worry over a little film of dust. Besides, I read and reread all my books and when I take one down, I wipe it off. Doesn't that count?

I like my drapes open and the windows clear to view God's world around me. So many things go on in nature. I don't want to miss a hummingbird scavenging for spider webs to build her nest or a bright yellow butterfly dropping by for dinner from the lobelia.

I have a collection of bird houses, incense burners, pots of dried weeds, baskets of homemade pot-pourri, Native American artifacts, and books. And yes, they're all dust catchers. But all of this *stuff* is a collage of my life. How can I throw away my life?

~~~~~

I wonder if Anna Reeves Jarvis realizes what she started when she told her followers to write Mother a special letter to observe a special day. Or if Woodrow Wilson knows what has happened since he declared Mother's Day a national holiday. He even authorized government officials to display the U.S. flag on all government buildings and invited citizens to put out flags at home as a "public expression of our love and reverence for the mothers of our country."

Receiving a card, gift, or phone call is anticipated with excitement. And mothers around the country are disappointed if the message is not received.

Have you noticed all the objects adorned with the words, "World's Greatest Mother?" I would like to send a message to the manufacturers and designers of these items that this title is a poor choice. I am not the world's greatest mother.

I made many mistakes when I was raising my children. I gave too much discipline at times and not enough discipline at other times. I smoked while I was pregnant. I fed them fatty foods, eggs, and sugar. I didn't hug enough. I stifled their independence by standing over them like a sentinel, fearful that they might take part in some activity that would cause them harm.

I warned them if they were disciplined at school they would get double restrictions at home. I made them wash dishes, fold clothes, dust, clean the toilets, dump the trash, and mow the lawn.

When they were old enough to drive a car they were forced to get a job to pay for their own gas and insurance. They had to be home before curfew, and sit at the table every evening and eat dinner as a family. I yelled "no" instead of practicing "time outs". I never told them it was all right to do what they felt like doing, thereby hindering their creativity. I didn't say "I love you" every day. And, yes, I confess, I spanked.

So according to today's standards I have not been a good mother. And even though my kids are successful despite my parenting skills, the therapists have won. They have taken my self-esteem as a mother and smashed it on the rocks of modern psychiatry.

Therefore, the accolades on this important day must go to those women who deserve them. Those kind women who adopt the unfortunate and give them a loving home.

To all those childless women who mother us all; the dental assistant who held my hand because I was frightened; the nurse in the hospital who was nurturing and caring; the ladies at my bank who are always helpful and patient; the truck-stop waitress who gave a lonely man a pat on the back; the neighbor who came at once when I called.

Perhaps it isn't in their lifescript to have children of

their own. Perhaps the plan is to leave some women free to mother all of us when we are frightened or sick or lonely.

No matter how old we grow, we all want the perfect mother; someone with an ample bosom to hug us when we're depressed; a woman who smells of home-baked bread and oatmeal cookies; a saint who has all the answers, protects us from all adversity, and is always there.

To all women, Happy Mother's Day and thank you for your kindness, patience and understanding.

ꞈꞈꞈꞈ

For memory has painted this perfect day
With colors that never fade,
And we find at the end of a perfect day
The soul of a friend we've made.
                               Carrie Jacob Bond

I went for a walk this evening. The warm, soft summer dusk had descended over the valley.

Night insects were beginning to rouse from the dewy grass and hung in the air like dust motes.

A dog barked in the distance.

Faraway, a child called, "Coming!"

The doves, one by one, flew into the trees to settle down for the night.

A strong aroma of earth and sweet alyssum enveloped my senses.

The sun had set in the west and a full white-rose moon hung in the east.

The black fir trees were silhouetted against the purple sky as a breeze riffled through their branches fluting a ghostly tune.

A spider was alert in the center of its lacy kitchen, waiting for dinner.

Suddenly, it was dark! Stars blinked with cool anticipation. Crickets began their twilight serenade. The splendor of the evening had passed. But I gave thanks for the moment, because precious moments like these are fleeting.

I wish each of you could have walked with me this evening. It was a time to share. We could have quietly given thanks together for a flawless moment freely offered just for our pleasure.

But I thought of each of you and I knew you would have been as grateful for this moment of tranquillity and serene introspection as I was.

≈●≈●≈●

My husband put up a swing in my Open Garden. He built it according to my specifications. I wanted a flat, unpainted board with holes drilled through the seat where a clothesline rope was to be attached. Then I wanted it hung from a tree limb where I could sit, swing, and dream.

Being an engineer, Bob brought out his draftsman's tools and began to draw up grand plans, but I insisted that I wanted a simple board swing like the one I had when I was a child. That swing had been a weathered gray board that swung from ropes tied to the apple tree in the orchard where the earth beneath had been trenched away by small feet. It was years before anything would grow in that spot.

So, despite all Bob's engineering logic, he cut the board and drilled the holes. He did insist upon weatherproofing the seat with varnish. And, of course, the ropes are nylon. "Stronger and weather-resistant, you know."

He climbed the ladder and tied the ropes with seaman's knots to the thickest branch of the tallest tree in my Open Garden. Now I sit and swing and ponder the day's happenings. Tranquillity overcomes me when I glide on my swing with my fingers curled around the ropes and my feet swinging free.

I am once again a child waiting for Mom to call me to supper. I can hear Dad chopping weeds in the garden then sighing and plunking the hoe against a tree. I can smell the purple wisteria and the windfall apples fermenting in the tall grass beneath the gnarled old tree. I hear the steam engine chugging through town on its way to exciting places. The cicadas call my name and June bugs slap against the screen door. For a few moments life is lazy, free, and innocent.

I wish everyone could have a tree with a swing hanging from its branches.

ॳॳॳ

I spoke to several young people who are not familiar with the meaning of Memorial Day. The only thing Memorial Day means to them is a day away from school.

I also learned that they have never heard of Adolf Hitler or the Holocaust; have never done in-depth studies on World War II, the Korean War, or even the Vietnam War.

And I wonder if they are aware of the men and women who died during this century so they would have the freedom to learn what they want, to say what they want, and to wear what they want.

Why aren't they being taught about the outrages Adolf Hitler perpetrated on innocent people? Why aren't they being taught about Mussolini? Or Hirohito or Tokyo Rose? Why don't they know about the Bataan march or the atrocities committed in the prisoner-of-war camps of Japan, Germany, Korea and Vietnam?

It's a grave mistake not to teach these horrors. For those who forget are doomed to repeat. We must never forget the young men who slept in muddy foxholes, or lost their arms or legs or eyes so we could write what we want, say what we please, and go where we wish. Each of these patriots sacrificed their lifescript so we could follow ours.

We must raise our flag high and instill a sense of pride of country in our youth instead of denigrating America and her leaders at every opportunity.

And perhaps learning about the arrogant Hitlers of the world would benefit our children more than memorizing what year the American Revolution was fought, when the Boston Tea Party occurred, or how many lanterns were lit in the church steeple the night of Paul Revere's ride.

ᘓᘓᘓ

June

Singing Cricket Moon

*W*ell! Here we are in our golden years. Those years of freedom we've planned for since we were 40 years old. We never plan on retirement before 40 because we know when we're young that we'll never grow old. Suddenly, at 40, aging enters our minds. We see those first feathery lines forming around our lips. We find those first gray hairs. Webs of blue veins begin to appear on our thighs. Our buttocks sag just a little. We become depressed with reality as our savings account balance chases away all our idealistic plans.

But we know it won't be all bad. We begin to save money and plan ahead for those joyous moments when the empty-nest syndrome we were warned about passes and leaves us as free as we were when we were teenagers.

Settled now, we play golf, travel, and stay up as late as we choose. The house only needs to be dusted weekly because nothing is ever out of place. We eat delivered pizza or a bowl of canned soup and toasted cheese sandwiches.

We read in the quiet of the bedroom, work in the garden, sleep late, and mow the lawn that finally has grass growing over the makeshift softball field that had been worn to muddy ruts by years of sliding small feet. And then we get the call.

"Mom and Dad? I was wondering if I could move back home? It'll only be for a few months."

We shove papers into boxes and stack furniture in the garage as the spare room, turned into a comfortable hideaway years before, is transformed back into a disheveled bedroom.

Half-empty diet soda cans now decorate the coffee table, mantel, and book shelves.

Déjà vu takes over as we search for the scissors, pens, and cellophane tape.

Friends can't reach us by phone. Loud music cracks the walls. The bathroom is always steamed up and sticky from hair spray. The washing machine is never empty and the dryer is never cool. The driveway is glutted with cars, and people come and go at all hours. Shoes and socks litter the living room floor, potato chips are ground into the carpet and our old dog hates the new cat.

If I could locate the individual who first expounded the theory that the empty-nest syndrome was traumatic, I would stuff the crumpled candy bar wrappers, the discarded sweaters, the snooze alarm, and the cat's litter box right up their thesis.

❧❧❧❧

*W*hen I was a kid, most men worked an eight hour job. When they came home they mowed the lawn, fed the chickens, hoed the garden, repaired the roof, and pruned the trees. They worked on their car, stoked the furnace, chopped wood, milked the cow, and went to church every Sunday.

Children assisted with the outside chores and the inside cleaning. They went to school daily, attended church on Sunday, did pages of homework every night, and in their leisure walked the woods, swam in the stream, picked wildflowers, and played games.

Women canned vegetables and fruit, baked bread, cooked a full course daily breakfast and dinner, packed lunches, cleaned the house, washed the clothes in a wringer washer then hung them out to dry. They ironed everything, tended the children, and sewed all the family clothing. They dressed chickens for Sunday dinner and volunteered for church activities.

These men and women still found time to sit on the porch on summer evenings and sip lemonade. They related tales of the past and hopes for the future as they listened to the crickets and watched the lightning bugs flashing in the meadow.

Why are the people of today so busy? Where are

they going when they're dashing here and there? Even housewives maintain an appointment book to remind them of their upcoming engagements. Freeway traffic moves at a dervish pace. Fathers spend all their time earning money. Mothers can barely find time to throw a box into the microwave.

Children can no longer be children. They're never permitted a moment of free time to lie on the lawn and daydream. Every second must be filled with activity. The freedom of spontaneity has become old fashioned and being busy has become a status symbol. It makes me wonder if all the labor-saving devices and modern technology have been worth the price.

Wouldn't you like to take all these people aside and tell them that the most valuable activity they can do is to sit on the porch on a warm evening, sip lemonade, and make small talk with family or friends?

When they're old and can no longer keep up the frantic pace of activity, will they have learned how to rejuvenate their body and spirit?

Will they have any memories of security and calm?

Will they wonder where the lightning bugs have gone?

❧❧❧❧

I never expected to be a kid again! I never knew I would one day go about my business with the same abandon as before the weight of grown-up responsibilities settled on my shoulders.

Since I'm older, I'm recapturing my childlike humor—that giggling, silly, uncaring, unembarrassed joy.

I'm comfortable. I can safely flirt with young men, tell silly stories, sit on the floor and play games, nap by the fireplace, stay up as late as I want, talk on the phone for hours or sleep till noon.

Every moment now is precious. So rather than waste time in a beauty shop, I wear braids, pony tails or play dress-up with a French twist.

I sit on my garden swing and watch the clouds.

One day, my neighbor called through the trees, "What are you doing? Day dreaming?"

I smiled and said, "No. I'm looking for castles and gnomes."

A look of shock flittered over her face as she turned away.

Undaunted by public opinion (or a neighbor's glance), I bury my face in an opened watermelon and eat its sweet red heart. I walk the fields and find beauty in nature's bounty, build snowmen in the winter's cold, drag home stray puppies, dress in my witch costume to cackle at trick-or-treaters, or get up every hour to nurse orphaned kittens.

My bedroom is as disheveled as it was when I was a teenager. There are more important things to do now than polish furniture, wash windows, or scrub floors. It no longer matters if my appliances match or if the pillows are fluffed. Instead, I watch a woodpecker walk upside down on a tree trunk or follow ants as they carry giant parcels. I'm in awe of rainbows and I search the lawn for four-leaf clovers. And when the sun lowers its iridescent curtain on the day, I watch the moon rise and wish upon a falling star. I'll make that wish come true, because wishes change with age, too.

Our society looks forward to every age except old age. When we are children, we're anxious to be teens. When we are teens, we can't wait until we're twenty-one. When we're in our twenties, we plot and plan for those settled years of our forties when we'll be established in a beautiful home with a loving spouse, ample savings and two cars in the garage. But oh, how we all dread the thoughts of becoming old!

Throughout life I always seemed to live according to the rules drawn up by society. Suddenly, here I am in my golden years! This is my final opportunity for one, last, great hurrah! I will hurrah according to my rules. Society's rules be damned!

❧❧❧❧

*J*une is the month when we honor our fathers. And although I had great difficulty, I finally came up with a few words about my dad. After all, what can one say about a man who never did anything spectacular during his lifetime?

He was a blue-collar worker and an avid Cleveland Indian baseball fan.

He was French. He was liberal.

He never disciplined any of us children, much to my mother's chagrin. Occasionally he tipped too many glasses of homemade wine.

He swore a lot, chewed tobacco, and thought anyone who was sophisticated was somewhat immoral.

He never gossiped.

He worked every day even during the depression and continued working a few days each week after retirement.

He grew wonderful summer gardens filled with acres of corn and tomatoes; cucumbers and pumpkins.

He pruned all the trees into perfect shapes and knew exactly which branches to remove and which to leave alone.

He went to church every Sunday.

He liked his food fried in deep fat. Mother was German and preferred boiled food so there was an occasional supper eaten with dissension.

On the first day of every December he placed two saucers on the mantel for my sister and me. If we were good, the next morning we found a gift from Santa; a piece of hard candy or a penny. If we were bad, the saucers remained empty. These Santa visits continued daily until Christmas morning.

He looked forward to picnics, Christmas dinners, and any affair that included family, friends, or neighbors.

He played euchre with the locals; and when he was older, he pestered any visitor until they agreed to a game of checkers . . . and then another . . and another.

His motto was, "Everyone and Everything Must Earn Their Own Keep."

There's nothing more I can add.

He was just always there.

&&&&

God cast aside all inhibitions when He created the woods. They are almost decadent with the sweeter things of life. And there is no other place on earth that shares its spirit quite so abundantly as a sun-dappled woods on a sultry, summer afternoon.

The cool breeze hums through the shadowy trees. Flying squirrels soar overhead. Birds sing. A raccoon peeks drowsily from its tree-trunk den. The pulsating sounds of the brook lulls one into a sensual calm as it bubbles over the smooth rocks. Frogs plop into the stream as soft footsteps interrupt their naps. The leaf-strewn floor is carpeted with purple violets, blue forget-me-nots, and yellow cowslips. Voluptuous skunk cabbage thrust their strange stalks out of the leafy mold. Small gray mice dart beneath a fallen tree. Thick, moist, deep green moss covers the tree trunks and mushrooms attached to the trees' damp bark are sculpted by nature into giant, dusky crescents. A snake slithers through the sparse grass as birds scold from the treetops. Muskrats are busy renovating their watery homes. Time stops. Worries end.

Woods, unlike forests, are filled with colorful

hardwoods and flowering shrubs. Many woods are small enough for a person to spend a languid afternoon walking from one end of the copse to the other to find a surprise nestled behind each tree.

Even the winter woods are covered with a white silence that permeates the setting and makes it overflow with serenity. The only sounds are from the restless stream or hungry birds looking for dried seed pods that the leafless trees have stored to share.

But the summer woods are best. When entering the confines of the shaded hideaway, an invisible silk curtain descends and seals out the humid heat, creating a private paradise.

A huge tree, fallen across the stream, creates a natural footbridge. Solid and wide, one can walk part way across then sit with bare feet dangling in the cool water, watching for a gnome to dart from behind a tree or a faerie to step from beneath a bush to dry its gossamer wings as the enchanting interlude continues. The clear stream, running free, exposes freckled fish searching for dinner, while green, iridescent dragonflies perform a ballet across its surface.

The beguiling woods are God's masterpiece of mystery, sensuality, and abundance; a spellbinding oasis created, then tucked away in a quiet corner where anyone can go to dream in uninterrupted solitude while observing the hidden life that thrives in the untroubled, subdued neighborhood enclosed within a raucous, cluttered human world.

Summer

"Drifting in a sultry day on the sluggish waters of the pond, I almost cease to live and begin to be."

Henry David Thoreau

July

Full Thunder Moon

*W*ho says I'm old-fashioned and opposed to new ideas?

After all, I've heard about tortellini. I went to the supermarket and after a lengthy search through the pasta aisle, I found the tortellini in the refrigerated section.

I rushed home, dropped it into a pot of boiling water and waited. And waited and waited and waited. It seemed an hour had passed before I drained it then poured it onto a platter where it bounced and rolled like the tires off a plastic truck.

Undaunted, I grabbed the package of tofu. After trying every recipe in the tofu cookbook, I surrendered. I threw the crud (I mean the curd) into the trash along with the book.

Those no-calorie rice cakes were next. I decided they were a freak of manufacturing and fed them to the birds.

Finally I conceded that some of the new foods were not my cup of tea. I turned on the television to prove once and for all that new can be better. I watched a few sit-coms, but I couldn't stop laughing at the wardrobes long enough to follow the sketchy plot.

I switched on the music video channel. I was incapable of correlating the scenes with the lyrics which consisted of a few lines repeated endlessly. After a momentary lapse of sanity, and a case of vertigo brought on by the flashing pictures, I switched to the talk shows. All the guests were involved in a shouting match, and I couldn't understand anything anyone was saying. To settle my nerves I drove to the Mall.

I wandered through a jewelry store and discovered the weight of the gold nugget rings forced my hand to hang like a plumb bob at my side.

I went into a leather shop and tried on some jackets. I looked like an NFL player in drag.

At this point determination became my companion. I went into a shoe store but only found replicas of the shoes that were stored in the attic when I was a child.

I drove home and walked to my garden. The roses smelled the same as they had 65 years ago. Bees hummed the same tune; butterflies flew the same flight patterns. And I learned that being old-fashioned is very satisfying. Familiarity breeds contentment.

I have two dogs—two little dogs—both Cairn terriers named Tish and Mac.

They're annoying, create a mess and have caused an unending amount of inconveniences in my life.

When people visit, the terriers know these guests must be dog lovers and have surely come just to visit them. Mac leaps onto their laps, licks their faces and wiggles with joy. Tish dances about their feet and whines for a pat on the head, then rolls over for a tummy rub.

They bark! A high pitched, incessant nervous yapping at cats, birds, cars, sounds (imaginary or real) and at any stray dog that may be patrolling our fence.

They have accidents on the carpet and occasional gastric upsets that result in the emptying of their stomach contents on the best rug—often in front of important guests.

Tish is frightened of thunder. She pants loudly until every family member is ready to be institutionalized. Mac is frightened, too, but his is a silent fear. He jumps on my lap and trembles until the dangerous sounds dissipate.

They detest grooming, baths, or nail trims. When they see the equipment in my hands, they run and hide. As a result, grooming is not as frequent as it should be.

Treats must be eaten on the carpet not the linoleum. They dribble water on the floor outside their water bowl, sleep in doorways and shred tissues throughout the house.

They have a path worn around the edges of the backyard, and in the flower beds bury bones which they decide to recover only after I've planted new, tender seedlings.

They're always on the wrong side of the door; they either want outside or they want inside.

Though not litter mates, they've been together since they were 6 weeks old.

They were 15 years old this past April. Time is growing short. What will Mac do if Tish goes first? What will Tish do if Mac goes first? And what will I do?

Who else will greet me with cries of pleasure when I come into the house after being gone just a few minutes? Who else will keep stray cats out of the yard? Who else will tell me when someone is knocking at the door? Who else will clean up every crumb I drop on the floor? Who else will lie at my feet for hours while I write?

Like best friends, their faults have been outweighed by their good qualities. And I'm sure there's a special place prepared in Heaven for little dogs who spend their lives giving so much love, loyalty, and joy. There has to be.

❦❦❦

*R*emember when we were kids and we had to write one of those awful essays "What does America mean to me?" and we all came up with the same old trite plagiarized words copied directly from the Declaration of Independence or the Preamble to the Constitution?

Now that I'm older I have a different perspective on the topic of America. I realize today that being an American is not only having freedoms and rights and equality and justice but being an American has also given me the right to make mistakes.

Americans are the most envied people in the world, perhaps because we can get on with life the way we please. We can rail against the government openly without fear of recrimination. We can demand retribution.

Edward Everett Hale in *The Man Without A Country*, quotes Philip Nolan, *"Remember . . . that behind all these men you have to do with, behind officers and Government and people even, there is the Country Herself, your Country, and that you belong to Her as you belong to your own mother. Stand by Her . . . as you would stand by your mother!"*

And so what does America mean to me?

America is going to the supermarket and coming home with a car filled with Florida oranges and Texas lettuce and California berries and Idaho potatoes.

It's deer browsing in our forests.

It's flags and ice cream socials and backyard corn roasts.

It's fireworks and protesters at the White House.

It's elections, country fairs, jazz, and mountain

songs.

It's covered wagons and sod huts and golden wheat fields.

It's the right to peacefully assemble to disagree about everything from wars to roosters crowing in the neighborhood.

It's fiddle players and concert masters.

It's flowing rivers and willowed streams.

It's generosity and compassion.

It's the right to debate another person's belief no matter how un-American, and standing by one's convictions no matter how undemocratic.

Even though we take America for granted, we must remember with every blatant dissent we espouse, every flag we burn, every failure we survive, every lost soldier we mourn, every corrupt politician we endure, she will continue to be the land of the free because she is also the land of the brave.

I am grateful to have lived my life in a country that bestowed on me the right of passages my way without fomenting retaliation from my government; a country that protected my right to succeed or fail; a country that protected my right to be what I wished; a country that protected my right to worship according to my beliefs. Amazingly, I did nothing to earn these privileges, they were given to me without fanfare on the day I was born in this wondrous land called America!

And so it is that I stand by Her . . . as I would stand by my mother!

ჼჼჼ

$\mathscr{T}$he stages of intelligence present an interesting study in irony.

When I was 14 years old, I knew I would never be wiser than I was then. I knew everything about everything; and if I didn't know, it wasn't worth knowing. If, by chance, someone quizzed me on an alien subject, I expelled a loud sigh, rolled my eyes and retorted, "Geeeez! That's really a stupid question!"

Suddenly I was 18 and my IQ had risen at an alarming rate. I was even more intelligent than I had been at 14. There was no stream I couldn't cross; no mountain I couldn't climb; no problem I couldn't solve. After all, I *was* a college freshman.

Then one day I turned around and 15 years had vanished! Mornings were spent changing diapers and slathering peanut butter and jelly across bread. Afternoons were whiled away reading about hasty bears, little trains that could, and digging jacks out of the shag carpeting. Evenings were spent at PTA meetings, Girl Scout Jamborees, or Little League games.

Then in a haze of prom dresses, football injuries, and pizza boxes I discovered my IQ had diminished. I knew because I was reminded daily that I just didn't know what was going on out there in the real world.

Now I'm in my 60's, and I have lost my comprehension abilities. I can't figure out which item goes into which recycling container; grasp which foods contain too much cholesterol; master which side of the tape goes into the player; get a grip on how to lace my athletic shoes, or solve the puzzle of my granddaughter's car seat. I suspect my IQ has plummeted to zero.

Today, when I could use all that intelligence, I don't have it; and when I had it, I wasn't allowed to use it. Therein lies the irony.

And I spend many of my days lamenting the loss of that 14-year-old whiz kid who vanished years ago. With her IQ, one that would put Mensa Society members to shame, she could surely teach me how to do percentages on my calculator, unravel the new simplified Yellow Pages, explain what a modem is and, with a grumbling sigh and a roll of her eyes at my ignorance, demonstrate how to open a can of charcoal lighter fluid.

❧❧❧

"But though an old man, I am but a young gardener." Thomas Jefferson

So it is that I am young once again when I'm in my garden. The wind in my hair, mud on my boots, the sun on my back fills my soul with calm and my body with peace. To dig and feel the earth sift through my fingers brings memories of the sand castles and mud pies of my childhood. It evokes the same feeling of abandon I experienced as a child riding my tricycle down the sidewalk.

Even seed catalogs bring the same indecisiveness as standing before Mr.Burns' full penny-candy jars lined up on the worn wooden counter.

Lawns are a nuisance, but my garden is a sanctuary of pleasure—my Eden—a dear companion.

Gardens blossom with joy, disappointment, and success. They are home to bees and faeries, butterflies and wasps; food for the eye and the body— teacher of lessons no school can offer.

Cottage gardens show mistakes and precision; geometrics and free-flowing patterns just like life, filled with the unexpected. Venerable lilacs still blooming by rotted cabin doors are a reminder of the permanence of gardens.

Man can find his true nature in his garden. He can see himself for what he is. He will learn that the more diligent he is and the more connected and loyal he becomes the greater will be his harvest.

The younger generation can keep their sweaty gyms and stuffy tanning parlors. I will bask in the sun as I bend to weed, breathe the fresh air as I twist to rake, and smell nature's goodness as I stretch to prune. And my reward will be the bird's song, the bee's hum, and a sun-warmed tomato, seeds dribbling down my chin as I sit on the bench under the old locust tree and savor God's gift to man.

It is only just that a feeling of security and abundance should overwhelm us as we dig and plant and wait for life to push up through the soil and envelop us with the childlike quality of immortality.

All people need a garden where they can contemplate their roots, nourish their souls, and glimpse the essence of paradise.

❦❦❦

*J*uly is the month when many of us celebrate our roots. Towns plan parades that promote themes of Frontier or Pioneer Days. Women dress up in sunbonnets and calico dresses. Men grow beards and wear suspenders on their black woolen pants and straw hats on their heads. They play horseshoes and eat corn-on-the-cob while the children stumble through potato sack races. Ladies keep the groaning tables stocked with food, and everyone is filled with laughter and joy.

Men were and are born adventurers. They yearn to travel unknown paths. But women? Women were born for security—roots. And it's those pioneer women who must never be forgotten.

How many of us would survive if we were faced with traveling the prairie riding in a bumpy wagon or walking in the wind and mud beside exhausted horses? How many women do we know who are capable of building a fire of sticks then cooking the family supper night after night in a pot hanging over a smoking pit? How many of us could beat our laundry on a rock and rinse it in a stream? How many of us could face the loss of one child after another and leave their little bodies under a pile of rocks far from home?

To those women who walked the dusty trails in their hot woolen skirts and long petticoats and lived in sod huts and bore their children in beds that rested on dirt floors and cooked rabbit stew and gathered dried berries for pies and grew wrinkled and old at 30—I salute you! You must never be forgotten.

Your perseverance was the start of our California dreams, the beginning of the Nevada gold mines, Kansas wheat fields, Washington apple orchards and Oregon gardens. You are our heritage—you filled us with life and determination.

Every fire that you built of buffalo chips; every pie that you baked with shriveled berries; every quilt that you stitched from scraps; every loaf of bread that you baked over coals; every bucket of water that you carried; every dirt floor that you swept; every flower that you nourished with dishwater; every trip to the outhouse with a sick child; every unattended tooth-ache you endured must be remembered by us—your offspring.

For without your stout-hearts our lives would not be what they are today. I thank you women for my inherited knowledge to recognize that life is what I make it, and I honor you for giving me the intelligence to implement that knowledge in my day-to-day living.

♨♨♨♨

August

Full Peach Moon

*W*hy is it that I can keep my house dusted, the kitchen floor waxed, the bathrooms sterile, the lawns mowed, the throw pillows fluffed, bowls of fresh flowers on the tables, a chocolate layer cake decorating the counter top and no one visits?

But on the day I'm schlepping around in my slippers and robe, hair frizzed out to here, the kitchen floor dotted with mud balls from the terriers, beds unmade, sink filled with dirty dishes, bathrooms littered with wet towels, the furniture looking as though it had been dusted for prints, and not one scrap of decent food in the house, a car drives in and unloads touring, distant relatives I haven't seen in 3 years?

Not wanting to appear mean-spirited despite the fact that since I'm older I detest surprise guests, I weakly tell them how happy I am to see them, then praying against all odds for the correct response, I politely but foolishly invite them to spend the night. Naturally, they accept with joy! And I discover that somewhere down the line people became misinformed about seniors. They seem to think if you're retired and over 60, you're definitely lonely and will simply love to have folks just drop in.

Nervous and inattentive, I sit and talk while I'm thinking about beds to be changed, a dinner menu and breakfast. Good grief! Breakfast!

Surprise guests are one thing, but guests for breakfast? Never! There's something private about mornings. Mornings are personal time. I don't want to be polite to guests at 7 a.m. I need time to wake up, drink my coffee, watch the birds, walk through the garden, read the paper, then get dressed and plan my day. I don't want to make morning small talk. Especially morning small talk with unplanned visitors.

Upon leaving the next day my visitors assure me they came just to see me—not the house (so they *did* notice the cobwebs hanging like party festoons), and they realize it *was* last minute (the ring in the tub?), and next time they'll take me out to dinner (the creamed burger on toast?), and they'll even make plans to stay in a motel (I forgot to take the litter box out of the bedroom!), but they always fail to mention that there will be no more surprise visits!

We hug three or four times as they gather up their belongings, and I even begin to feel a little guilty over the three-day-old cinnamon buns I served for breakfast. We wave good-bye, and I dash back into the house and begin to scrub and dust. I even bake a chocolate cake. Insurance, you know.

❧❧❧

A funny thing happened to me on the way to my golden years. I learned about priorities!

Too many times in my youth my priorities were misplaced. I actually read boring bestsellers. I spent hours at proper functions that were not enjoyable. I went shopping or lunched with the wrong people for the wrong reasons. My house was sterile. Windowsills dusted. Throw pillows fluffed and placed precisely in the corners of the couch. Area rugs properly aligned. Crystal sparkled. Silver polished. Our clothes were folded then arranged neatly in the correct drawer. Clean towels were hung daily in the bathrooms. My floors would have put Mrs. Cleaver's to shame. Even the junk drawer was straightened monthly. My kitchen was color coordinated. The bedrooms had matching sheets, spread, drapes, and pillow shams. The children were ordered to keep their rooms neat, beds made, and clothing picked up.

And then, one day, I read a remark by Helen Hayes. She said that she found as she grew older that time was too important to waste reading a bad book. She explained that if she didn't enjoy the first page she threw the book aside. Since the day I read Miss Hayes' remark, I began to alter my lifestyle.

I discovered that excitement had been passing me

by. I was missing the beauty of living. I was forfeiting the wonders of life for unimportant minutiae. The true meaning of existence had been buried beneath layers of years wasted on frivolous matters. I awoke to the fact that I was spending my life the way society expected me to live rather than living my life the way I wanted to. And now, since I have learned to set priorities, life is joyous!

I've learned that it is more important to hand-raise an orphaned kitten than to clean the refrigerator. My time is better spent walking through my garden admiring the snapdragons than spending that time making the bed. Silk flowers aren't as beautiful as a bouquet of dried weeds in the old crock on my dining room table. The hum of the air-conditioner isn't as soothing as the soft southern breeze blowing through my opened front door. Un-waxed floors, dotted with tufts of cat hair, won't wear out any faster than highly polished floors.

My rumpled home wraps me in warmth as I sit before the fire, sipping tea, reading Emerson—no longer agitated by disorder.

This evening, even though the kitchen table is dotted with bread crumbs, and a large dollop of tomato sauce has dribbled onto the cloth, the sun, settling below the horizon, won't wait. I toss down my napkin, and the terriers and I dash outside. The western sky is ribboned with pink streamers. In the north a clump of gray clouds are edged with gold. I know, as I watch twilight's closing act, that tomorrow's show will be new—different.

I pick a plum, clean it on my shirt, pop it into my

mouth, and wipe its juice from my chin. I settle down on an old stump and while the terriers play at my feet, wait for the moon to rise in the east. The crimson glow cast over the earth fades to a colorless silver gleam. The evening is still. A cricket chirps. The first star twinkles and then another. Soon the Milky Way glows a path above me. Satisfied, I turn toward the warmth of my home.

I'm grateful for growing up. Maturing. For aging! I've finally learned to enjoy all the wonders so freely offered. Wonders I had never seen before. Wonders I had cast aside. Wonders I had always considered unimportant—until now.

❧❧❧

*M*y little Tish died last week.

My blond, fluffy, feisty Cairn terrier who had been a part of my life for 15 years didn't rouse Saturday morning. I found her in her blue bed by the back door when I entered the kitchen. We chose her gravesite out in my Open Garden where she can keep watch over the backyard and all the comings and goings. Mac, her little gray companion, misses her as much as I. They had been together since they were 6 weeks old.

But I catch glimpses of her now and then. Once I saw her sitting by the back door, her smiling face looking up at me. Another time I saw her dart across the lawn after a blackbird that was stealing food from her dish. And I hear her. On Tuesday when I walked through the gate, I heard her speak to me. Just a faint, quiet "woo-

woo-woo." And when I write, I hear her sigh as she shifts sleeping positions at my feet.

Tears at the death of a companion are necessary to purge the grief that is so potent when one loses a dear one. Words of sympathy are welcomed but they can't soothe the aching heart we must endure.

I have found that one must mourn alone because emotions are personal—each of us must deal with the pain of loss in our own unique way.

I still have my little Mac. And even though he's deaf and nearly blind, he grieves, too. He always went to bed willingly every night. He'd crawl into his cozy, brown bed and curl up and snore. Now he's hesitant about going into the kitchen alone. He misses Tish. He misses dancing across the lawn with her and barking with her and eating with her and sleeping with her. He no longer begs for his treat every morning. But Mac and I will be all right. We know that one day we'll see that little honey-colored body gleefully bounce across silvery, dew-struck grass to welcome us home.

❧❧❧

*B*ugs and I don't get along too well. Of course, I have total respect for all living things; however, bugs are in another category.

Now don't get me wrong, I know that bugs have their proper place in the environment, but that place is not in my house or on my body! And bugs have a penchant for always trying to be in places where they have no business being.

Here, on the desert where we live, we have bugs, lots of bugs. Ants apparently spend their lives in the process of reproduction. We have big ants, fuzzy ants, teeny ants, red ants, black ants, brown ants, and even furry white ants. And most of them bite; a painful, burning sting that hurts and itches for hours.

We also have black widow spiders. They like to hide in dark recesses where they build their homes. After I became familiar with a black widow's web design, her secret was out. She builds random webs that are as strong and shiny as fish line. Just walking into a sticky web is a frightening experience because it adheres to the skin like glue. Of course, you know that Momma is on her way to attack whatever damaged her home, so panic sets in rapidly.

Widows are nocturnal and hang in their webs like shiny, black beads. Her sac is virginal, white cotton-like material that belies its contents, and she protects it as ferociously as a mother bear protects her cubs.

I have been bitten twice by black widows. The bite is painless, but the grief arrives later. The first time I was bitten I became sick, very agitated, and was left with a silver-dollar sized welt that turned from red to purple to green to yellow.

The second bite resulted in the same symptoms along with blood poisoning that sent me to the doctor for a two weeks' regimen of antibiotics.

We also have scorpions, wolf spiders, earwigs,

slugs, snails, fleas, ticks, and dozens of other creepy crawly things that are nosy, under foot, and very unwelcome house guests. And I don't mind any of them as long as they tend to bug business and stay out of mine.

I spend a fortune on bug sprays, granules, and powders, preferably those with residual powers so bugs who like to sneak around behind my back will pass on to bug heaven.

We also have termites. They attack any piece of wood that is in contact with the ground and this includes picnic table legs, so both of my picnic tables are elevated on concrete blocks to ward off the damage done by these voracious little pests.

There are a couple of bugs I like. I like crickets, and when I find one in the house, I wrap it in a tissue and carry it to the garden. We also have a small beetle called click-beetle. It sits in the trees at night and clicks coded love messages to its mate. Its song, along with the cricket's, is a comforting sound. Ladybugs are another little bug I like. They don't bite, they eat aphids, and tend to ladybug affairs. The only time ladybugs come into the house is when they hitch a ride on laundry that has been hung outside.

I also enjoy butterflies although I don't consider them bugs. They're more like independent people intent on finding the sweeter things of life. They mind their own business as they visit all the garden flowers. (Some people say we don't have as many butterflies as we once did, but I suspect that's because grown-ups just don't take the time to look for them.)

Anyway, the other day I was busy in the garden when a yellow jacket decided that the flowers on my blouse were overflowing with succulent nectar. Now we all know that it's foolish to bat at a yellow jacket. But none of the bug experts have ever explained how one can retain a calm demeanor when a yellow jacket is determined to settle down for dinner on one's shoulder. They just refuse to get the message and become irate at the very suggestion that they are unwelcome pests.

I screamed and batted. The armed scoundrel grew alarmed and dashed in for the kill. He darted up the leg of my shorts and stung me on my you-know-what! I couldn't sit comfortably for days.

Experience has taught me that bugs don't seem to have much intelligence. If they did, they'd have learned by now that they may live in peace in my garden, woodpile, or garage, but my house is not the proper environment to build a bug nest or to raise bug families nor is my body a bug landing field. But experience has also taught me that bugs are persistent, so my penalty for bug persistence is swift and severe. Works great, until one of them retaliates with a kick in the pants.

❦❦❦

I've been camping three times in my life. And since I'm somewhat of a slow learner, that's why it took three outings before I learned that camping was not my favorite activity. In fact, I would rather scrub the toilets, wash the garbage cans, or scoop out the cat's litter box than go on another camping trip.

My first experience with camping occurred shortly after my husband and I were married. He surprised me with a weekend camping trip to the upper peninsula in Michigan.

We left late in the day and arrived in the backwoods about midnight. Bumping and thumping along dirt roads that had obviously been used for land mine practice we went deeper and deeper into the foreboding depths of the forest. We finally arrived at the "perfect spot," unloaded our gear, set up the tent in the dark, and crawled into the sticky, flannel-lined bags for a short night of unrest.

"What was that?" I asked when a crashing sound echoed through our makeshift home.

"Just a branch falling," my husband said.

He couldn't fool me. I knew that a bear being chased by Bigfoot was about to stampede through the flimsy tent flap and crawl into bed with us.

Soon, I also discovered I was not able to master the art of a fishing reel (I grew up with a bamboo pole, hook, and worm). I didn't like my eggs sprinkled with wood ash, and a bush or a hole in the ground did not, in my opinion, qualify as a designer bathroom.

The second camping trip began with a modern little camper about the size of an outhouse, similar to the one Humphrey, of the comic strips, pulled. We went to Vancouver, British Columbia.

With this sophisticated rig we had to park along

the road at night. There were no rest stops then. I knew we would be attacked at any moment by a gang of mad rapists in search of a sitting duck.

This up-to-date rig was not, in the vernacular of camping enthusiasts, self-contained. After much maneuvering and backing up and going forward, we finally got parked in a farmer's pasture. I was pregnant at the time so you can visualize the embarrassment involved in those repeated trips to the big house on the hill.

However, the most amazing thing was that I quickly learned that while my husband went out fishing every day, my day was spent in abject boredom. I wrote letters and read books while I scratched mosquito bites. Of course, this free time was not available until after I had scrubbed the tiny floor, wiped off the wobbly table, washed dishes in the toy sink and made the bed by falling across the mattress to tuck in the sheets. Only then could I use my spare time to write postcards wishing they were there rather than me.

On the way home we hit roads under construction, and everything in the trailer spilled onto the floor. We spent a week cleaning it up before we returned it to the rental agency.

The third and final lesson included our three small children and a site in the High Sierras in California. We went in August, but when we arrived at the campsite and turned on a spigot, ice clinked out of the tap into our cups. We determined that the heat from a Coleman lantern, circa 1963, did not produce enough warmth for five quivering bodies huddled inside a canvas tent. We formed a ball of flesh as we wrapped around each other and drifted off into a shivering sleep. And then the baby threw up.

When I arrived home, our humble little cottage looked so welcoming and warm and clean that I wanted to hurl myself against its walls, hug it, and tell it that I had finally learned my lesson; I would never again complain about its small rooms, lack of storage space, or smoking fireplace.

Now, every time I see a motor home slowly wending its way along the byways, with a bumper sticker that states something about spending the kid's inheritance, I envision a woman passenger, her head covered with a cute little hat that hides the fish scales in her hair, bowed in a silent prayer. She's making a vow to never grumble again about a backed-up sewer or dog hair on the couch if only God will find a way to make this motor home collapse on itself as it sits in the driveway.

❧❧❧

September

Gray Owl Moon

Our daughter, married 10 years, was due to deliver us our first grandchild. We were overcome with joy.

We shopped for toys, clothes, and furniture. The baby's layette was complete three months before she was born. At our home we were prepared for visits with a high chair, playpen, and crib. I bought diapers and powder and lotion. I crocheted blankets and sewed pads.

All our friends told us what pleasure we would derive from bonding with our little darling. We could barely wait!

And then the big day came, and our delightful little pink and white bundle arrived. Tears welled in our eyes as we beheld this miracle of life.

I spent the first week with Mom and Baby. While Mom recovered, Daddy and I took turns on the night shift. We changed diapers, fed, rocked, sang, and cuddled.

Finally Baby reached the age of awareness. One day she looked at Grandpa and Grandma (us), bellowed hysterically, kicked spastically, and clutched at Mother's shoulder. Tears flowed down her cheeks.

Her mother remarked, "I've never heard her cry so hard," reinforcing our feelings that her rejection was aimed only at us.

Grandpa took off his glasses and hat, but it didn't fool her. We were outcasts. A tiny, 12 pound, three-month-old child had reduced us to demonic beasts who eat babies for lunch.

Even though we were active in her life, she continued to shun us. All our plans and hopes were lost in a grim fairy tale.

After months of cajoling, playing, and assuring, we have become an acceptable part of her life.

The trouble with bonding is that we read all the books and understood them to mean the development of a close relationship through mutual friendship and love. But the baby hadn't read any of the books. Her definition of bonding was one of imprisonment by trolls who live under a bridge. But it worked out all right. We found that grandparenting can be very rewarding when the bondee cooperates with the bonder.

❧❧❧❧

Lost, yesterday, somewhere between sunrise and sunset,

Two golden hours, each set with sixty diamond minutes,

No reward is offered, for they are gone forever.
Horace Mann

*T*he older one grows the more valuable time becomes, yet we all waste so much of it. We are spend-thrifts of years. Days burn holes in our pockets. Hours are lost as minutes dwindle into nothingness. We allow seconds to pile up like dead leaves waiting to be raked and burned to ash. And when we reflect on the past, we mourn those squandered moments with more regret than goals unattained or lost loves.

Time is a jewel offered to us to do with as we choose, and if we could begin again, not one of us would leave that jewel unguarded.

I suspect all of us would walk through more gardens, read more, and love more. We would share more with family and be more giving of ourselves. We would maintain an open door policy for friends. Careers would merely be a vehicle. Money would be necessary only to survive comfortably. Hurrying would become obsolete. We would never alienate loved ones or spend time with those who refuse to accept time's importance.

But it's not too late to salvage the precious time that remains in our lifescript. We, of all peoples, know how short life really is. We must not fritter away another day on the pain of hate, the sorrow of loss, or the regret of what might have been. We still have time to make amends to others and to repair any damage caused to ourselves by our extravagance.

Time is our most precious commodity, yet it can't be bought or sold. Time is, as Mann said, *". . . golden hours, each set with sixty diamond minutes."*

⋇⋇⋇⋇

*W*hen they say children are a blessing in our old age, did they mean because when they leave home they leave behind their aged pets and half of their belongings?

Our closets are filled with broken toys, piggy banks, dolls, and unreturned library books. When we suggest they be removed, thrown away, returned, or given away, we are met with resistance.

"Hang on to them. I may want those someday." Or, "Oh Mom, I can't go through that stuff now, I'm too busy!" and "I don't have room to store those things."

Occasionally they dash into the house and declare, "Gosh Mom, this kitchen sure needs to be painted," or "Gosh Mom, you really need to update this room and get rid of some of this junk!"

Please understand, I'm not complaining, but also remember these remarks are coming from someone who once thought a tuna can ashtray was just the ticket to decorate the coffee table, and a Reader's Digest Christmas tree, spray painted green, was a beautiful, sophisticated addition to the center of my dining table. And let's not forget all those tissue boxes covered with globs of glued macaroni that adorned the mantel.

Last month I had a garage sale. I advertised "30 years of stuff." The kids helped out and said, "Well, thank heavens, you're finally getting rid of all this junk." But as box after box was emptied and spread out on the tables we had set up in the driveway, mutterings began.

"Oh-h-h, I remember these. I really don't want to sell them," she said as she held up a pair of '70's hip-hugging bell bottom trousers.

"I remember this old radio. It was my first one. I think I'll keep it. It probably just needs a battery."

"Hey! That's my Girl Scout flashlight."

"Good Heavens, Mom. If we don't keep an eye on you, you'll be selling the kitchen sink," they said after noticing the Lego set they'd received from Santa in 1965.

"Mom," one whined. "This is the pencil holder I made for you out of Popsicle sticks when I was in the first grade. You're not getting rid of it, are you?"

After I assured them that I had loved and appreciated and used all the wonderful items they had made for me, I thought I'd convinced them it was time to move on. Skeptically, they eyed me. Then I noticed they each had a box set aside filled with their precious memories. When they left, their memories thankfully went with them and are now gathering dust in their closets.

However, we still have one old dog who needs medication twice daily, two old cats on special diets, and a vacant horse stall rusting away out by the back fence.

⁙⁙⁙

*W*hen I go shopping, I often suffer a state of depression when I remember the thrill of browsing through the 5 and 10's of my youth.

The uneven wooden floors, the mingled smells of popcorn, hot dogs, chili, and peanuts wafted throughout the store. Canaries sang, dishes rattled, and cheery conversations filled with laughter as the phonograph at the front of the store played the latest records. *"I'll wa-alk a-lone, for to tell . . ."*

Soldiers and their girlfriends giggled as they exited the photograph booth.

There was always something I could afford; a seashell necklace, a leather coin purse, a lace handkerchief, a bottle of 10¢ nail polish, Flame Glo or Tangee lipstick, a colorful snood, or Lady Esther face cream. When I was really in the money I always purchased a sheet of music with a song that was popular.

"Harbor Lights," with a lonely lighthouse on its blue cover, cost 35 cents.

There were yard goods, combs, buttons, hair pins, and candy scooped up into little, flat white paper sacks.

In the summertime the front doors stood open emitting tempting aromas from the lunch counter and the trill of Ted Weems whistling "Heartaches."

Every section was staffed by a young girl with red lips and rouged cheeks; a bright flower pinned in her bleached hair. Each clerk demonstrated her merchandise with bored aplomb, bagged the purchase, and graciously thanked each customer.

Shopping alone was best. I could take my time as I nibbled peanuts and examined the displays. Part of the time was spent in the record booth listening to the latest hits and deciding which record to buy. The rest of the time was spent in the magazine or book section.

When paperback books came on the market, I'd sneak a peek at a few risqué lines in "God's Little Acre" or the latest Mickey Spillane book, knowing that if I spent 25¢ on either it would be found and destroyed the moment it entered the house. I'd study the pictures of the beautiful, forlorn women on the cover of "True Confessions" wondering what their love story would reveal. I knew I was not permitted to read these bawdy tabloids, but temptation is the middle name of all teens.

Finally, purchases clutched in my hand, I'd climb aboard the bus for the trip home. When I arrived, I'd dreamily play my new record of "Sentimental Journey," take a bath in Blue Gardenia bubbles, apply my red lipstick, pin a white celluloid rose in my hair, and feel confident that I had a wonderfully romantic life ahead of me.

❧❧❧❧

I haven't understood anything since 1960.

Rock music assaults my equilibrium. While shopping I'm boom-boxed about the ears. I had always believed Congreve's remark: *"Music has charms to soothe a savage breast, to soften rocks, or bend a knotted oak."*

I was ill-prepared for the wardrobes that have appeared in public that have been scrounged from Aunt Hattie's rag bag. And cars! What about cars? All I need in a car is one that looks decent and gets me from here to there. I don't need a power antenna or a seductive voice that tells me about the status of my keys, brakes, gas level and seat belt.

I can't operate the VCR, digital clock, or set a watch. I don't understand how fax machines or computers work. I can't even figure out how to lace my Reeboks.

Even operating the lowly washing machine, microwave oven, and dishwasher requires a degree from Silicon Valley to decipher the garbled instructions.

Eating is trying my very soul. Does it have cholesterol, fat, sugar, sodium, preservatives, additives, and taste?

Our vocabulary has changed. We no longer have stewardesses, we have flight attendants. Chairman has become chairperson. We can't date but must be involved in a relationship with a significant other. Dumps are landfills. Going for a run has become jogging. Doing a few jumping jacks is called aerobics. And if it's bad, that's good.

Antibiotics have been christened with names that include every letter of the alphabet. When I visit my doctor, he speaks in tongues. When I ask for explanations, I am told not to worry.

What does solid state mean? What is software? Is it the opposite of hardware? What about call-waiting and cellular phones? I really don't care if people get a busy signal when they call me, and thank God I don't have a phone in my car! Someone would probably try to talk me into getting my carpets cleaned as I tootled down the freeway.

I don't understand why women shave off all their hair or why men grow theirs long. And why would anyone want a ring in their nose or their belly button?

I always heard that little boys are made of snips and snails and puppy dog tails, but I thought that was just a childhood nonsense poem. I never expected to actually see them sprouting tails on the backs of their necks.

I can't begin to comprehend a 4 trillion dollar deficit. I worry if I charge $100 on my credit card.

And what happened to accidents? We are living in an era of no accidents. It's always someone else's fault. People sue friends, strangers, neighbors, even family members.

I am drowning in advice from 30-year-old experts. They tell me how to be a grandmother, when to exercise, how to look younger, what makeup to use, how to treat arthritis, and when to retire—all this after they tell me what a terrible parent I was.

But I know something they don't know; I'm going to live until I die. And I'm going to do it the old-fashioned way, by finding the humor they offer in this modern world of day-to-day living.

❧❧❧

It's difficult to accept aging as a natural process when we are inundated with questions or remarks that remind us daily of our battle with gravity and the passage of time. Perhaps we're too sensitive. Perhaps we're reading something into these questions and suggestions that are not there.

"When you die I want that."

"Mom? What causes those brown circles all over your hands and face?"

"They had that when you were young?"

"Why doesn't Grandpa have any hair?"

"Would you like to apply for the senior discount?"

"You used an outhouse? How gross!"

"You shouldn't be climbing a ladder. Falling at your age can be very dangerous."

"Yuk! Why are your toenails so thick?"

"Gee! I hope I don't get long hairs on my chin when I'm old!"

Then there's television. Advertisers point out how unattractive gray hair and wrinkles are, and recommend an expensive way to get rid of them. They use a twenty-year-old cutie with collagen-injected lips pouting words of wisdom as to how we could look if only we'd use their products. They drive home the fact that our age group is not only constipated, but that we stubbornly maintain that only home-baked pies are fit to eat. And, of course, we all know that soup must taste as though Mom just dressed the chicken in her backyard and tossed in some carrots she pulled from her garden.

Just when we have finally passed the age when we are no longer embarrassed to make purchases of personal items at the drug store, we are advised that now we will need to buy huge packages of costly padded undergarments to hide another private problem.

Stand-up comedians portray us as doddering, interfering old fools who talk with a toothless slur, wear ill-fitting pants pulled to our chests, limp, and can't function properly in their busy, intelligent world. Our only redeeming value is to give them material for their routines.

Our mail is littered with throwaway junk about life insurance, burial plots, spending the equity in our homes, and protecting our pensions. However, it does give one confidence to know that all those folks out there, who don't even know us, are so concerned about our retirement portfolio.

Then there's the doctor's visit. A mild feeling of malaise will bring the retort, "Well at your age it could be almost anything so I think we'd better do some Xrays and blood tests."

And the dentist is filled with advice on root canals. At the slightest pause he threatens us with dentures. "And, of course, dentures are not like having your own teeth," he laughs, exposing a perfect plate.

So, no matter how often we are advised to think young, eat young, dress young, and act young, we are never allowed to forget that we are growing older. But that's all right. So are they.

❧❧❧❧

Autumn

"We have lived not in proportion to the number of years that we have spent on earth, but in proportion as we have enjoyed."

Henry David Thoreau

October

Full Pumpkin Moon

There are so many lessons I have learned throughout my lifetime, and I wonder, on occasion, why I didn't know them when I needed to know them. Such as:

- Moving doesn't bring happiness.
- Planting one hill of squash is sufficient.
- Cleaning house is a waste of time.
- Weeding is never done.
- Bare spots in the lawn are not a blight on the world.
- A bad haircut will grow out.
- A roof over one's head, food in the stomach, and a warm coat really are all we need.
- Fallen soufflés are a minor inconvenience.
- No perfume is as fragrant as a kitchen aromatic with homemade bread.
- Sauerkraut is not rotten cabbage.

- Weather reports cannot be trusted.
- I will not have to pay for someone else's sins, or be rewarded for someone else's goodness.
- It's not easy to fry a perfect egg.
- I'm responsible for my own entertainment.
- A batch of burned cookies is not a major catastrophe.
- Aging is beautiful when accepted with grace.
- There's no way to get too much salt out of a pot of soup.
- The best things in life really are free.
- There is nothing as valuable as a dear friend.
- House plants are too much work.
- Education requires more than reading lots of technical books.
- Vinegar does not take the odor of dog urine out of carpets.
- Money really can't buy happiness.
- Tofu does not taste good no matter how it's served.
- It's foolish to eat anything that burns the mouth or throat.
- There was no need to memorize all those historical dates in grammar school.
- Restaurant hamburgers always taste better than home-cooked burgers.
- Dogs know more about loyalty than humans.
- Life is meant to be lived on a daily basis rather than letting it pass us by while we plan our future.

❧❧❧

*I*t really doesn't matter to me what society says, or feels, or thinks about aging. What really matters is what I know about aging. And I know that I never looked better than I do now.

My face, rather than vacant and empty, bears lines of living. All the sadness and joy I have experienced circles my eyes and lips and is etched across my brow.

I can pile my hair atop my head and forget about mousse, dye, and sticky sprays.

I have learned which colors suit me best, which shoes are most comfortable, and which coats are the warmest.

I have developed a self-assured attitude I could never have attained at 20, 30, or even 40 years of age.

I discovered bravery I didn't know was contained within my soul. I feel I could take on the world and win. I'm tough and thick-skinned and no longer become incensed at ungraceful remarks delivered by disadvantaged others who have never found the pleasures in life.

I enjoy being alone now because I like myself. It pleases me if that sounds arrogant, because I have learned that one of the first attributes to dissipate with age is the sense of arrogance. Too many of us lose our feelings of self-importance. We allow ourselves to be devalued. My generation is a generation that should maintain its arrogance, for after all, look at what we have given the world.

And I find now that being alone brings pleasure rather than a debilitating need. I can write, think, work in the garden, or tear up the house and put it back in order next week.

Like a sunflower, my face always turns toward the warmth of sunlight. And I have learned the importance of stopping throughout each day to brush mortality from my shoulder and smile at this gift of life presented to me every morning when the radiant dawn pours across my pillow signaling new beginnings, new opportunities, new life . . .

❧❧❧❧

*W*hen I was a kid, I had convictions! I knew just what I would be like when I was an old woman.

I wasn't going to let myself go. I would always wear high heels. I'd never even consider putting Cuban heels or flats on my feet. And I would never wear those ugly floppy slippers that all the older folks wore.

I'd never wear loose house dresses, tie on an apron, or let my hair go gray. I'd wear jewelry every day, have my hair done in the latest style, and I was not going to get those unattractive brown spots on my face and hands. I would exercise, thereby avoiding sinewy legs. I'd not permit my body to develop varicose veins, wrinkles or thick toenails.

I'd never be intolerant or lose patience, I'd retain my sense of humor, never worry over insignificant problems or watch political conventions.

I'd never lock my doors because I knew that everybody had goodness in them. I would always be able to leap out of a chair without grunting and groaning. I'd drive the speed limit and never get nervous in heavy traffic.

I'd always be interested in the latest movies, scandal magazine trivia, and keep my nails painted with the latest colors.

Under no circumstances would I be an out-of-date complainer about what kids are doing these days. I would be a moral liberal. After all, people had values; they would only go so far.

I'd be active. I'd bounce and bubble my way through old-age. I'd lie in the sun to keep tan and then snip a rose and pin it in my hair.

I'd shun crocheting, nonfiction books, and crossword puzzles. I'd avoid classical music and only listen to the latest hits.

I'd never find pleasure in cats or gardening.

I'd always be able to eat steak, corn-on-the-cob, crisp apples, peanuts, and chili—and I'd never be called "Grandma."

My kids would drop by every day and we'd sip tea while discussing the joys of living. My house would always be clean and ready for guests.

Did I stand by any of my convictions?

Sure I did. I don't wear aprons.

Autumn is my second favorite season of the year—only surpassed by spring. Autumn brings pleasant weeks when a tinge of cool air huddles around the edges of the days. The smell of windfall apples and the heady scent of ripening grapes are intoxicating.

Now the October sky is a brilliant blue dusted with white puffs, rather than the pewter blue from summer's heat. I sit on the porch and watch the birds gather into flocks as they prepare for their flights to warmer climates.

Pumpkins shimmer silver in the fields under a voluptuous moon. The whisper of leaves falling in the quiet of the night brings moments of alarm until the sounds are recognized. Mats of pine needles carpet the woods. Grasses have been spun into gold.

There's a harmony to the seasons that brings balance to our lives. Autumn is the start of a quiet time; a time to slow down, a time to sit before the fire, sip tea and read. With charm and grace it becomes a subdued, sophisticated, operatic season that brings with it arias of cool breezes that hum through the fir trees. And that charm is welcomed after the frantic rock n' roll beat of summer's torrid afternoons when we dashed to the ball park, hoed the garden, mowed the lawn, planned backyard barbecues, swim parties, and picnics at the lake.

Autumn is my time to make up for all the sins of omission that occurred during the summer. All those it's-just-too-hot-to-do things I should have done and didn't. It's a time to rake away all the dead leaves and put the roses to bed. It's a time to fill up the shelves with jelly and the freezer with summer's bounty. And it's a time to cleanse the soul before the long, cold winter sets in to discourage me from repentance. Best of all, autumn brings Halloween, my favorite holiday of the year.

Fire-red woods glimmer behind fields of orange pumpkins as excited kids prepare for the big night. And I, childlike, prepare too. I carve the pumpkins, decorate the porch, and leave a welcoming light lit even though we never have any goblins knocking at our rural door. But each year I stand at the window and watch, and I'm filled with the hope that some brave child will wander down our lane and timidly tap on the door, then shout "Trick or Treat!" After all, hope is what the change of seasons is all about.

So, on my evening walks with the terriers as the cool night air settles across the valley, I watch the Full Pumpkin Moon rise in the east and pray that all people will always be filled with hope, for without hope there is no faith and without faith there can be no charity.

༄ༀༀༀ

Attaining the ultimate art of letting go can be pure bliss as we age.

I'm not referring to all those important events that happen in everyone's life such as grief after losing a loved one or those feelings of guilt over omissions we all have endured. Rather, I refer to all those insignificant plans and thoughts that molded our youthful excitement as we plotted our future.

I've learned to let go of vanity and ego and that self-righteous attitude of youth that pertains to the valuing of people, including myself, by outward appearance. And I learned that to envy others of their material wealth is not only tiring but a waste of emotional time.

On hot days there's nothing more comfortable than a loose shift that touches my rounded body nowhere except my shoulders. I no longer have the desire to wear tightly belted skirts or sleek pants. I've discovered that as my waist thickens my need to look svelte recedes. I've let go of all that "what's in" hoopla. I choose not to waste time in a beauty shop having my thinning hair done. It looks fine (and thicker) piled atop my head. Comfort has become primary as I shop for low-heeled shoes.

I now have the freedom to refuse all those highly seasoned foods since I know full well that my stomach will revolt. Of course, my stomach revolted when I was young, too, but my ego prevented me from admitting that fact.

I'm no longer interested in all-night parties, hobnobbing with the correct people, making my fortune, or becoming famous. I've happily let all those fantasies dissipate as surely as the sun settles beneath the horizon. I'm now armed with common sense; a sense that often escaped me during my younger years.

I've finally learned how to love myself with all

my imperfections. I no longer care what others think. I'm comfortable wearing my own shoes, and have discovered that another person's shoes will never fit me.

Today, my life is written across my face. Laughter, sorrow, joy and grief have all carved their initials upon my cheeks and around my eyes. When I look into a mirror, instead of lamenting my lost youth, I give thanks for these reminders of the strength that was given to me to see me through.

I've discovered that letting go was the beginning of pleasant days filled with serenity. And, unwittingly, serenity was exactly what I'd been searching for all those years.

ɹɐɹɐ

One of my greatest regrets as I age is that I have no stories handed down to me from the women of my past; ladies of my mother's generation never told their secret thoughts or desires. They didn't speak of past indiscretions, hopes, fears, or sorrows. They never told tales of what their own mothers had hungered for. Had they been happy? Had these women been content to live in the shadows of their husbands and their children?

Men, on the other hand, were free to talk, to tell their stories—stories that were embellished with each narration. They laughed as they bragged and rehashed their youth. Their women sat, pretending interest. Well rehearsed, they laughed in all the right places, showed

shock or horror in all the right places and acted embarrassed in all the right places. And I wondered what
yarns these women had locked away in their own private memories.

What had they hoped for their future when they
were young? Did they have goals? Did they want to
be a dancer instead of a quiet wife? Did they give up
opportunities to become tired mothers who spent their
time canning fruit in a stained apron? Did they want to
drive a car and go to parties and dance the night away
rather than ride the street car to town to shop for material to sew a new dress or shirt for their children?

Men could be bawdy as they sipped their wine
and smoked their pipes while their modest women
dashed from stove to table. And these women stood
mute as they listened to their men recount their exag-
gerated tales of what could have been, what was, and
what might still be.

Did these women want to make lye soap, dress
chickens, crochet rugs, stand over a coal stove cooking jelly on hot summer days, rock babies, and wear
the same "best" dress Sunday after Sunday?

On hot August afternoons while they ironed, did the
steam rising from the dampened clothing carry whispers
of sunny beaches, or fragile remembrances of what
might have been? Did it carry vague ghosts and gray
shadows that quickly evaporated into the murky air of
forgotten dreams?

While the men boasted of their skills at playing
ball, farming, hunting, or their cleverness at a recent

business transaction, their women washed dishes and set the table and mended socks and quietly peeled potatoes.

My mother would sit with her eyes closed, hum softly and rock in the rocking chair—a dim smile on her face. What was she remembering? When she sat up until 2 in the morning sewing feed sacks into bed sheets, what thoughts were enclosed within her secluded recollections while the household silently slept?

When meals were served at our house, my father was always given the meatiest pork chop and the crispiest potatoes. The desserts were desserts he preferred. And I wondered now and then if Mom would have liked the best pork chop, the one with the thick white tenderloin, succulent and sweet, instead of the thin chop that had curled over and dried out in the frying pan.

Uncomplaining, she would say, "Give the nice chop to Papa, we'll eat these others."

But, sometimes, I still wonder what Mom was dreaming when she sat in her rocking chair late at night, eyes closed, a bittersweet smile playing around her lips as she softly hummed, *"After the ball is over. After the break of morn. After the dancers leaving. After the stars are gone. Many a heart is aching, if you could read them all. Many the hopes that have vanished. After the ball."**

ﭭﭭﭭﭭ

*Chas. K. Harris/ *After The Ball.*

November

Red Leaf Moon

$\mathcal{R}$ecently, I have been wondering why no one whistles anymore. I remember my brothers whistling as they chopped wood or mowed the lawn. Men always seemed to be whistling as they walked down the street. Boys practiced whistling until they had refined their tunes to a perfect art form. They stood in front of mirrors, puckered up their lips, and blew until they had attained the proper whistling look.

The habit of whistling is a happy habit, showing a carefree spirit and a contented heart. Men don't even seem to whistle at girls anymore. We called it a "wolf whistle." Now the young men rudely hoot, call obscenities, or polish their fingernails across their chests. And although we girls always pretended to be offended by the whistles, there still seemed to be a game of repartee that passed between the whistler ("you are gorgeous") and whistlee ("thank you very much").

Perhaps men today feel so much pressure from the strain of keeping up with the Joneses and pursuing a successful career that they no longer feel lighthearted enough to whistle?

Whistling produces such a merry sound, a bit of whimsy that brightens our day. Everyone, whistler and audience, benefits from listening to this happy, gay melody. It sends one into another world of carefree abandon where problems vanish and life is fun. Maybe if some of us would return to the joy of whistling we could reduce stress in our daily lives and many of our difficulties could be overcome by simply puckering up our lips and whistling a merry tune.

❧❧❧

*I*f I had my life to live over. . .
- I'd raise my children with less discipline.
- I wouldn't care what other people think—only what I think.
- I wouldn't wear anything uncomfortable no matter what the fashion experts say.
- I'd search for a warm little house and ignore the large cold ones.
- I'd have more dogs and cats.
- I'd look for answers by asking more questions.
- I'd be less critical and more forgiving.
- I'd gossip less, worry less and fuss less about unimportant things like clean houses, perfect hairdos and manicured lawns.

- I'd laugh more and cry less.
- I'd have more fires in the fireplace and not care about the mess.
- If I had my life to live over, I wouldn't be in such a hurry.
- I'd be more aware of time and more cautious about using it.
- I'd learn to play the harmonica.
- I'd take life less seriously and play more.
- I'd value friendships and spend less time with shallow people.
- I'd eat more peach pie.
- I'd send more valentines.
- I wouldn't worry about money.
- I'd plant more lilacs.
- I'd never wear black.
- I'd hug more.
- I'd build more snowmen, and watch more butterflies, and drink more hot chocolate.
- I'd measure success by my yardstick instead of society's golden ruler.
- I'd grow older but I'd never grow up.
- I'd read more, love more, and watch more sunsets.

If I had my life to live over.

৵৵৵

I'm a list maker.

I make grocery lists, gift lists, gardening lists, chore lists, guest lists, food-to-serve lists, and writing lists.

The value of lists is to help us remember things. I find it ironic that older people are accused of being forgetful, yet I've made lists since I was a young girl. The list-making habit hasn't changed, only the items. Now I've started another list, which I call a feel-better list.

Reading my feel-better list lifts my spirits on gray days and masks the pain of sorrows. It's a list of all those things I have always wanted to do but never even attempted, and it instills in me hope for my future. After all, a future without hope is a life that ceases to exist, so I'm going to share part of my feel-better list.

Learn to ride a bicycle.

Climb a mountain.

Tame a sparrow.

Mine for gold.

Learn to ice-skate.

Ride a horse to Alaska.

Hop a freight to nowhere.

Rent an amusement park just for me.

Stay up all night and watch the sky.

Learn to twirl a baton.

Dive for pearls.

Visit a haunted castle on the English moors.

Picnic on the Isle of Man.

Hike across Death Valley during a full moon.

Fantasy is not my cup of tea; therefore, I never write anything on my list that's not within my reach. Of course, I know that some of the things I've listed are highly improbable, but I've learned that nothing is impossible.

Some skeptics who have seen my list chuckle with the certainty that I will never accomplish any of the activities I have listed. But I know I will. And therein lies the difference.

❧❧❧

*T*his afternoon an acquaintance dropped by. The clouds had lowered and a cold rain was pouring from the eaves as I opened the door and invited my guest inside.

"Gladly," she responded. "It's awful out there!"

Pleased with my unexpected visitor, we sat for awhile before the fire, sipped a cup of vanilla tea, and carried on a philosophical discussion about the purpose of life.

She had read some of my columns that I had published under the title *Lifescripts*, and she was attempting to define the meaning of that word. We debated back and forth as to just what our lifescript was, when she stated that she felt that life is a series of sacrifices we are all destined to bear throughout our lives.

"First," she began, "we must sacrifice our ideals to please our parents, then we must sacrifice our freedom for our spouse, then we sacrifice all of our own material desires for our children, and finally, when we are old, we must sacrifice our health and our independence."

She paused for a moment, then continued, "Sacrifices are a cross that all women are preordained to carry throughout their lives." I disagreed! Sacrifice is not a word that is contained in my vocabulary and has never been part of my lifescript.

Each of us, man and woman, was given the gift of life with love, to love, and be loved. That is my lifescript.

I found the rain that cold, November afternoon to be serene, pleasant, and nourishing while my acquaintance found it debilitating and depressing. She may have also felt that she had sacrificed her afternoon to spend it with me.

ea:ea:ea

December

Full Snow Moon

*D*wight delivered wood last week. He brings us great logs, hewn from fallen trees found in the national forests.

I walk around these giant redwoods, awed by their size, and wonder about the history hidden in their rings and bark. The piney aroma they emit reminds me of campfires and pine needles, woods and nature. These trees have ended their lifescript, and now they will contribute to mine.

Before we begin to cut up the logs, I chip off pieces of the red, aromatic bark to add to my baskets of potpourri. Then my husband saws several thick slabs to be used as seats in my Open Garden. I prefer the natural wood for resting on rather than the chrome and plastic chairs available in the stores.

We cut and stack the wood ourselves and find this activity to be a humbling exercise. My husband slices the logs into manageable lengths then uses a wood splitter to separate them into fireplace lengths. As the pile of cut logs begins to grow, we carry and stack them. At the end of the day, pleasantly exhausted, we are rewarded with satisfaction and fuel that will last for months.

Dwight will suddenly appear, his truck piled high with uncut logs. Using the hydraulic jaws attached to the rear of the truck-bed, he snares each log with deadly precision and lifts it up until it spirals and dips—somewhat dangerously. Then Dwight releases the steel jaws and the log drops with a loud *thunk* onto the fallow area north of my Open Garden. After all the logs have been unloaded, Dwight silently crawls back into his truck, and with a great belch of burning oil spewing from its stacks, the truck lumbers back down the driveway.

We won't see Dwight again for months unless he has a problem with his truck. In return for all this precious wood, my husband keeps Dwight's ancient logging truck in a reasonably safe condition.

Dwight is considered by many people to be eccentric since he prefers the solitude of the woods and forests to the more urban setting where he maintains a home. He spends weeks in the high country, if not cutting and sawing, then looking over the terrain, getting permits from the rangers, checking out roads, and sleeping under the stars. I suspect Dwight is a very happy man.

On cold winter nights, logs crackling in the fireplace, I think of Dwight and the joy and pleasure he delivers with his venerable vehicle. A fire on the hearth offers memories of leisure moments shared wisely. I read the words of Henry David Thoreau and as I ponder his wisdom on life and nature, the feel of God's warm breath brings an afterglow of peace as fears fade into shadows, problems die with the cooling embers, and a drowsing calm secures the richness of life.

❧❧❧❧

*W*e hear so much today about the importance of commitment. We must make a commitment to our job, to our marriage, to our children, to our church, to our elected officials, to our country, and on, and on, and on.

Commitment sounds so cold, so regulated, so involved, so legal.

What's wrong with making a promise and sticking to it? Why can't we simply accept responsibility and carry it through to a successful end? Why do we have to refer to every promise as a commitment? When people marry now, they make a commitment. When they have children they make a commitment to raise them properly.

"A man is as good as his word," my father always said.

That's true. If you can't trust in a man's word, then that man cannot be trusted.

Of course, I'm still naive enough to believe people

when they tell me they will stop by to visit, or they will call me tonight at 7:30. I'm so naive that I will stay off the phone so I won't inconvenience them by having to place the call again and again because they got a busy signal. But they never call. Very few people today keep their word. Yet these are the very same people who espouse the value of commitments.

Commitment is a hollow word, a shallow word. Could we just begin to keep our promises and forget about the onus that goes with that word—commitment?

❧❧❧❧

*T*he other day I sat down and calculated how much of my time has been wasted during the past 60-something years. The wasted time added up to 13½ years! After the shock wore off, I made a pact with myself. I resolved that I would no longer permit anyone to waste any more of my life.

Figuring that there are 8,760 hours in each year and that I sleep 2,920 of those hours and spend 2,080 hours working, I balanced out the remaining hours spent on eating, recreation, television, personal care, business calls, shopping, playing with my grandchild and pets, and household activities. I still had 1,945 hours unaccounted for—11½ weeks each year. It was then I deduced those hours had been wasted. Where did they go? How could anyone waste nearly three months per year? Then I realized that I did not waste all those hours! Many of those hours—my hours, my time, my life, I had allowed to be wasted by other people.

How? Let me begin:

I have allowed others to waste my life by believing them when they said they'd call. I believed and waited in vain. Blithely, the next day, the culprit would brush it aside with, "Oh, I forgot. You didn't stay home and wait did you?"

I have wasted hours cooking gourmet meals that turned noses up to the chandelier.

Friends have wasted my life by repeatedly being late.

Doctors have wasted my life. All those hours waiting in the doctor's or dentist's office because my generation complacently accepted the fact that doctors were important people and their time was more valuable than ours.

Bank lines!

Motor vehicle lines!

Grocery checkout lines!

Theater lines!

Then, of course, all that time wasted waiting for children to come home, looking for lost items, and sniveling in bed with colds.

Time wasted listening to glib salespersons.

And when I tally it all up, I sadly discover that I have permitted 1/3 of my waking hours during my lifetime to be wasted! After my discovery I quickly implemented some changes.

Now, when I arrive for my medical appointment, I will wait one half hour past the appointed time. Then I tell the receptionist that she will have to reschedule my appointment because I can not wait any longer. I only had to do that a few times to learn that now when I arrive I never wait over 15 minutes.

I make every attempt to shop during non-busy hours.

All my banking is done by direct deposit.

I no longer search for lost items. Experience has taught me that they will either turn up or they won't.

When someone promises to call—I wait 5 minutes past the appointed time then proceed with plans.

I refuse to listen to sales pitches.

Of course, not all wasted time can be avoided. Being stuck in traffic jams, theater lines, etc. is still annoying, but I carry a book to read and don't feel quite so put upon while waiting.

Best of all, I learned through my time-study that I'm in control of my own life and my own time. I just wish I would have had this self-assurance (and knowledge) 60 some years ago. Who knows what wonders I may have accomplished during those 13½ years!

ða·ða·ða

Someone once asked me what I would do if I knew this was my last day on earth. The answer to that question has obsessed me many times over.

What would I do? I really don't know. I don't

think anyone could know the answer to such a complex question but . . .

I'll rise early to watch the sun welcome the day. I'll want to see again the rose-colored sky turn blue with new beginnings.

I'll spend a few extra minutes watching the birds eat from their feeders.

Then I'll climb a ladder and look into the hummingbird's nest.

I'll call my children and apologize for any mistakes I made and tell them once again how dear they are to me.

I'll lie on the grass and watch the clouds scud across the sky and dream them into a white horse to carry me off to paradise.

I'll make a fire in the fireplace, sip tea, listen to the logs crackle, and read an essay by Emerson.

I'll go for a walk and feel the wind on my face and gather up strange weeds.

I'll find sculpted wood that has been carved by time, then carry it home to put on the mantel.

I'll buy a watermelon, eat its sweet red heart and give the rest to the birds.

I'll walk through my Open Garden and bury my face in the lilacs to soak up enough fragrance to last an eternity.

I'll watch the western sky turn amber as the sun slides below the horizon.

Finally, I will once again lie down in the dewy grass and wait for the moon to rise in the east. Then

I'll mount my white horse and ride across the Milky Way and wave good-bye to an earthly life filled with joy, sadness, laughter and tears. I'll carry with me re-membrances of precious moments, and gratitude for the knowledge to have recognized their value when they came my way.

katkata

*I*n the small town in Ohio where I grew up, every-one knew everyone else. We all knew where everyone worked, their usual routines, every one of their family members, who was sick, who was pregnant, and who missed church on Sunday and why.

Strangers in our town stood out like a dirty sheet on a clothesline. And we all kept an eye on them.

All the parents in town were also my parents. If I misbehaved they scolded me, if I skinned my knee, any one of them would wash and bandage it and then take me home. If I succeeded at anything, they all were as proud as my parents. If I was frightened, I could go to any house in town and they'd take me in and pro-tect me.

No one worried about drugs or gangs; they wor-ried about polio and whooping cough. When some-one died, we all went to the funeral; and when some-one married, we all were invited to the wedding.

The entire town gathered together a few days after a young couple married and took part in "The Bell-ing" better known as a Shivaree. We all marched to the couple's new home late at night, stood on their lawn and banged on pots and pans and blew horns until they appeared and promised the town a big party the following weekend.

We all were involved in town picnics and church suppers. Religion didn't matter, nationality didn't matter, the only arguments were over politics.

And I've been wondering about all those people who cared so much for each other. Where did they go? What was I doing when they vanished?

Where are all those mothers in their house dresses and fathers in their overalls who raised me?

Where is their philosophy buried?

When were they replaced by onlookers who do nothing when someone is being beaten or attacked?

Where did all these people who feel no responsibility for other people come from? Who gave birth to all these young people without a conscience?

Where did the flag burners and bigots come from?

When did the longing for the Great American Dream become so great that it replaced human decency?

Donne said, " . . . *any man's death diminishes me, because I am involved in mankind; and therefore never send to know for whom the bell tolls; it tolls for thee.*"

I mourn the death of that small town, but mostly I mourn because no one bothered to toll the bell at its silent passing. And its death has diminished us all.

When I first moved to the desert of Southern California, I was certain I couldn't survive without red ripe peonies, sun-struck maple leaves, ice on winter ponds, thunderstorms, wild elderberries and cattle standing knee deep in green pastures. Summer came and went without crisp, fresh-picked roasting ears and juicy, tart tomatoes. Autumn came and went without colorful woods and air redolent with ripening grapes and bee-stung apples. And that first Christmas on the Mojave Desert was, indeed, blue. The season seemed out of kilter. It was sunny and warm. There was no snow, no sleigh rides, no snowmen. People even shopped in shorts.

My heart wasn't into picking out a tree or decorating the house with my usual frantic anticipation. I felt that my holiday spirit had been stolen and cast away on a dry desert mesa. How could the locals go about their merry business as though nothing untoward was going on?

How could they think their pathetic decorations looked festive on a background of sand? But I had youngsters who had made a list and checked it twice. They still believed in Santa and wanted a Christmas tree, turkey, and the traditional cake I make every year to celebrate Jesus' birthday. I had promises to keep despite my misgivings.

But then, one day, I remembered that the birth we celebrate took place in Bethlehem, probably in the month of May. A desert climate, just like mine, without snow, icicles, and all the trappings I had become familiar with in my Midwest home.

Suddenly the tumbleweed snowmen that decorated desert lawns appeared whimsical and creative rather than sad imitations. The wreaths hanging from the street lights no longer looked out of place, and the carols playing in the shops seemed appropriate.

I cut mesquite branches and decorated the mantle. Mums brightened the tables and we hung lights in the chinaberry tree that grew outside the front door. And suddenly, it was Christmas!

As we sat around the Christmas table, instead of thinking of all I didn't have, I silently gave thanks for what I did have.

No. I still don't have peonies, but I have fragrant poinciana trees. I don't have autumn colors bidding good-bye to summer, but I do have startling yellow and purple sunsets and brilliant rainbows that splash the sky from horizon to horizon. I have March daffodils and acres of April poppy fields. I don't have robins but I have a family of kestrels in my Open Garden and mockingbirds that sing me to sleep. I have juicy strawberries, big as eggs, and sweet oranges. I don't have great blizzards, but I do get snow every winter that stops by for a short visit and never wears out its welcome.

And it was at that first Christmas on the Mojave Desert that I discovered it doesn't matter where we live, because the Babe born in that arid region of Bethlehem, in a country called Judea, surrounds each of us with His beauty.

Christmas is not only a religious celebration and a seasonal celebration, but it is the only celebration that brings changes to the hearts of so many. The Star of Christmas shines on us all.

❧❧❧

About

Lois Erisey Poole

Lois Erisey Poole is a monthly contributor to 8 regional newspapers:

Elder Update, published by the State of Florida,
The Voice, Peoria, Illinois
Senior Views, Rogue River, Oregon
The Young at Heart, Lincoln, Nebraska
Over Fifty Magazine and
Past Fifty Magazine, Dillsboro, Indiana.

Her work was recently accepted by *O.L.D.E.R. Living*, a supplement to the *Tribune-Star* in Terre Haute, Indiana and *The Courier* of Rockford, Illinois.

Oblates Magazine has featured three articles.

Catalist Magazine has published two articles. One of her essays, "Finding Christmas," is published in **God's Vitamin C for the Christmas Spirit** (1996).

In 1994, she won the award for best humorous article from *Ohio's Heritage Magazine*. She has been syndicated by Clear Mountain Communications of Colorado and her articles have appeared in numerous newspapers throughout the United States and Canada. Her essay "The Freedom Years" was featured in *Golden Years Magazine* in 1990, and reprinted and featured in *Vintage Times* in 1991. She is also syndicated through the Senior Wire.

Lois has conducted several freelance writer's workshops in Northern Los Angeles County, and participated in round table discussions on writing personal essays. She has judged and critiqued student essays for the California Reading Association Young Author's Fair and was included on a panel at the Northern Los Angeles County 1996 Writer's Conference.

Personal

For two years in the 1950's, Lois had her own radio show and was a vocalist in local clubs. She and her husband, Robert, both retired, have been married 40 years and are the parents of three grown children. Lois was born in Ohio, and lived there until she was 26 years old. Her midwest ethics have always been an important part of her life, and an integral part of her writing.

She is a member of the Antelope Valley Writer's Network and a past member of the Palm Springs Writer's Guild.

Fans of her work may reach her in care of Pincushion Press at P.O. Box 3402, Quartz Hill, CA 93586.

Order Form

Ordered by:

_____

_____

_____

Ship to (if different from above):

_____

_____

_____

Name of book	qty.	price
Subtotal:		

Sales tax: add 8.25% for orders
from California   _____

Shipping: $3.00 per book   _____

Total: _____

Send check or money order to: Pincushion Press,
P.O. Box 3402, Quartz Hill, CA 93586-0402
or call 1-(800) 476-5758 with your credit card order.

Order Form

Ordered by:

_____

_____

_____

Ship to (if different from above):

_____

_____

_____

Name of book	qty.	price
Subtotal:		

Sales tax: add 8.25% for orders
from California   _____
Shipping: $3.00 per book   _____

Total: _____

Send check or money order to: Pincushion Press,
P.O. Box 3402, Quartz Hill, CA 93586-0402
or call 1-(800) 476-5758 with your credit card
order.

Order Form

Ordered by:

_____

_____

_____

Ship to (if different from above):

_____

_____

_____

Name of book	qty.	price
Subtotal:		

Sales tax: add 8.25% for orders
from California _____

Shipping:　$3.00 per book _____

Total: _____

Send check or money order to: Pincushion Press,
P.O. Box 3402, Quartz Hill, CA 93586-0402
or call 1-(800) 476-5758 with your credit card order.